Longman Keys to Language Teaching

Series Editor: Neville Grant

Visuals for the Language Classroom

Andrew Wright and Safia Haleem

Longman

London · New York

Longman Group UK Limited,
Longman House, Burnt Mill, Harlow,
Essex CM20 2JE, England
and Associated Companies throughout the world.

Published in the United States of America
by Longman Inc., New York

First published 1991

BRITISH LIBRARY CATALOGUING IN PUBLICATION DATA

ISBN 0-582 047811

LIBRARY OF CONGRESS CATALOGING IN PUBLICATION DATA
Wright, Andrew, 1937–
   Visuals for the language classroom/Andrew Wright and Safia Haleem.
   p. cm. – (Longman keys to language teaching)
   Includes bibliographical references.
   ISBN 0-582-04781-1 : $3.50
   1. English language – Study and teaching – Foreign speakers.
   2. English language – Study and teaching – Audio-visual instruction.
   I. Haleem, Safia.   II. Title.   III. Series.
   PE1128.A2W75   1991
   428'.0071 – dc20   90-42581
                                                                          CIP

Set in 10/12pt Scantext Century Schoolbook

Produced by Longman Group (FE) Ltd.
Printed in Hong Kong

Contents

Preface

THE *Longman Keys to Language Teaching* series is intended especially for the ordinary classroom teacher. The books in this series offer sound, practical, down-to-earth advice on useful techniques and approaches in the modern ELT classroom. Most of the activities suggested in these books can be adapted and used for almost any class, by any teacher.

One of the most important aspects of language teaching is the role of visual material: the importance of using visual media to make one's teaching more effective, communicative and interesting is well-known. However, many teachers – even experienced teachers – do not exploit the potential of visual materials to the full. In addition, deciding which techniques to use, for which language teaching purposes, is often problematical.

In this book, Andrew Wright and Safia Haleem survey the characteristics of the visual media commonly available to the classroom teacher – from the simple workcard to the chalkboard to the overhead projector (if we are lucky enough to have one). They show how, by appreciating the qualities of the different media, we can develop fresh and dynamic approaches in our classrooms appropriate for our teaching aims.

Like the other books in the KEYS series, *Visuals in the Language Classroom* is highly practical. It is full of interesting ideas on how to teach different aspects of language using visuals – and how to prepare them without fuss. Whatever we are concerned with – skills, or language content such as functions, grammar or vocabulary – fresh and practical approaches using visuals will be found in these pages. The book is also profusely illustrated – mainly by the authors themselves. The writers show us, by example, how we too can be as proficient as they are, not just in using, but also in making, our own visual aids. All the pictures in this book – and many others like them – can be produced with a minimum of time, money or skill!

Neville Grant

Introduction
To help you with this book

Visuals

In this book we have included all those visual media which are commonly found in the classroom or are readily available to schools and colleges. You will see by the illustrations in the book that we believe that the teacher and the students can make (simple drawings) or find (cutting out of magazines, etc.) most of the visuals needed. The only exception to this ready accessibility might be the overhead projector. What we hope is that the chapter devoted to the overhead projector will help teachers who do not have one to make a good case for having one.

The basis of this book

This book is first of all about the character of visual materials and how the teacher can exploit this character in language teaching. Appreciating the character of the media we use or which surround us (see *The learning environment*, Chapter 9) helps us to be more inventive, dynamic and efficient. So often the media of the classroom are used in a limited and dull manner – it is a little bit like speaking with a very limited number of words without intonation. It is such a pity and it is so unnecessary!

Artistic talent

It is obviously true that some people have a natural gift for being inventive and resourceful when using visual materials. However, most of the techniques and examples given in this book have been chosen because they require very little skill, time or money. Every teacher can do them! And, by the way, we have tended to choose examples which are straightforward and in many cases well-tried rather than emphasise the dramatic and eccentric.

Categories of activity

The activities are arranged under broad headings, such as:

Presentation (introducing language new to the student);
Controlled practice (you determine the patterns the students use but not necessarily what is conveyed);
Guided practice (you determine the general topic and give some guidance on sentence patterns to use);
Free communicative practice (the students make use of all the language at their command to express their ideas).

Obviously the degree of control will vary in each of these stages. Often, too, the four language skills – listening, speaking, reading and writing – will be approached in an integrated manner, so that work in one skill area will help work in another.

Mechanical versus meaningful language use

Manipulating language with little sense of meaning is of little value to the student. Most of the examples have been chosen to show that language can be used for communicative purposes even at the controlled practice stage. The underlying theme of this book is that, almost automatically, meaning and communication will be built into the English lessons by using visual materials.

Classwork, groupwork and pairwork

Lively language use for all students in the class depends on groupwork and pairwork. The bigger the class the more important this becomes. Many of the activities in this book assume that the class is divided into groups and pairs. Tips on the organisation of groupwork are not given here as it is well covered in other books in the *Keys* series such as *Effective Class Management* by Mary Underwood and *Techniques for Classroom Interaction* by Donn Byrne.

Questions and activities

There are many practical examples of how each of the media can be used in each chapter of this book. Furthermore, the structure of each chapter is similar. For these reasons, suggested questions and activities are grouped below rather than at the end of each chapter; most of the questions and activities listed below can be applied to any of the chapters of this book. The reader is invited to consider them while, or after, reading each of the chapters.

1 How would you decide whether or not an activity described in this book is suitable for you to use with one of your classes? Jot down about five criteria. If you are working through the book with other teachers, compare your five points with theirs. See if you can agree on a ranking of importance.

2 Compare your list of criteria for assessing the suitability of an activity with ours. There can be no final 'right' or 'wrong' list. See if you find any of ours useful. If you do, add them to your own list.
   Our list:
   ● Preparation time: if it takes a long time to prepare, for what you get out of it, then don't do it.
   ● Organisation in the classroom: if it is very difficult to organise in the classroom, then don't do it.
   ● Interest: if it is likely to be uninteresting to the students or if you feel you would be very uncomfortable doing it, then don't.
   ● Authenticity: if the activity makes the students use the language unnaturally, then don't do it.
   ● A lot of language use: if the activity passes all the above points but there is not much language used, then don't do it.

3 Take an example of an activity given in the book, think of one particular class of yours and apply your list of criteria to the activity. If the activity 'passes' the criteria quite well ask yourself if you will actually do it. If the answer is 'No', then try to establish what other criteria are preventing you from doing so. If you can locate and examine these other criteria your understanding of yourself related to the use of visuals may become clearer.

4 Referring to your criteria evolved in point 1 above, take any chapter and divide the examples into those which are the most suitable for one of your

classes and those which are less suitable. Compare your lists with the lists of another teacher (preferably one with similar classes).

5 The examples in each chapter have been chosen to reflect the special qualities of the medium. These special qualities are summarised at the beginning of each chapter under, 'Characteristics and techniques'. Select a few examples of activities from the chapter which you think best reflect the characteristics of the medium. Compare your selection with the selection of another teacher.

6 Select several examples from one chapter and write variations for them, perhaps for a different age and proficiency level. You can still retain the general idea.

7 Take some of the special characteristics of one of the media and try to invent some new activities. If you are working through the book with other teachers, after five minutes show your ideas to your neighbour. Work together on yours and your neighbour's ideas for ten minutes. Then the two of you join another pair (making four of you) and compile a list of ideas which you can then present to the class as a whole.

Note: Most people's minds go blank when they are asked to think of a new idea. Here are some tips:
- It is rare to come across something which is absolutely new, so don't expect too much of yourself!
- Be positive about any idea however trivial it might seem at first. Get into a positive frame of mind. Note down any idea that comes to mind, however impractical it might seem.
- Keep on imagining, using the special characteristics. Try them out in your mind's eye.
- Be positive about your neighbour's ideas. Concentrate on the seeds of an idea and of a possibility rather than looking for what is wrong with an idea.

8 An extension of point 7 above is to actually 'play' with the medium. In the act of handling a medium and exploring its character you might spot a new use for it. Chalk is dusty. In many ways this is a disadvantage. Can you think of any way, however minor, in which you might be able to make positive use of this dustiness?

Note: Merely reading this book is not enough: you need to try out the ideas in each chapter — experiment with them, as suggested in activities 7 and 8. This book tries to help by offering lots of examples, and, we hope, by serving as a source of inspiration for new or adapted ideas. However, until you *do* some of the things suggested, they will not really become your own!

Chalkboard and whiteboard

Chalkboards are found in most classrooms. They are usually black or green, cheap to install, easy and cheap to use and very adaptable. Some chalkboards are magnetised allowing pictures, word cards, etc. to adhere to the surface if magnets are placed on top of them.

Whiteboards are increasingly common though more expensive than chalkboards. Special pens must be used. Whiteboards are easier to keep clean than chalkboards; a greater variety of colours can be used and images can be projected onto the surface from a projector. The surface is often magnetised and even if it is not magnetised it is easier to stick pictures and cards to the whiteboard surface with sticky tape or adhesive plastic than it is to attach them to a chalkboard.

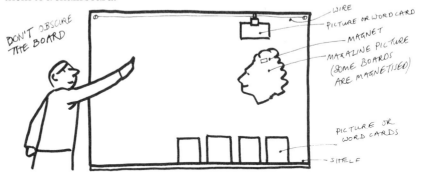

Characteristics and techniques

1 The whole class can see it.
2 Texts and pictures can 'grow' in front of the class.
3 Texts and pictures can be erased, added to or substituted quickly.
4 Parts of the board can be obscured.
5 Text or pictures on paper or card can be propped against the board, stuck to it or hung over it.

6 A white cloth or a sheet of paper can be stuck to the chalkboard or hung over it to act as a projection screen.
7 Several people can work on the board at one time.

This chapter now takes a number of aspects of the language learning syllabus, for example, tense, sentence patterns, vocabulary, functions and fluency and indicates how the special characteristics and techniques of chalkboards and whiteboards can be exploited to promote them.

Presentation and guided practice

The present continuous tense

Characteristics and techniques: drawings can be made to 'grow' in front of the class.

The present continuous tense (when it refers to an action which is occurring at the moment of talking) can be illustrated through the action of drawing on the board in front of the students. You use the present continuous to describe what you are doing as you actually do it rather than when you have done it.

Step one:

TEACHER: *(drawing a line)* I'm drawing a line.
(drawing another, line 2) I'm drawing another line.
(drawing another, line 3) I'm drawing another line.
(drawing another, line 4) I'm drawing another line.

TEACHER: *(indicating the first few lines of the stickman)* What am I drawing?
STUDENT: A man?
TEACHER: Yes, I'm drawing a man.
(drawing the line for the second leg and asking the question while drawing) What am I drawing now?
STUDENT: A leg.
TEACHER: What am I drawing now?
etc.

And finally . . .

TEACHER: What's he doing? He's running.
STUDENTS: He's running.

Step two:

Ask two students to be secretaries and to write on the board every verb of action the class can call out in three minutes. Then ask the secretaries to become artists. Ask each artist to choose one of the verbs and to illustrate it. The artists must keep stopping to ask the class what their drawing represents.

STUDENT: What's s/he doing?
CLASS: S/he's running/walking/swimming, etc.

Step three:
In pairs students draw on paper and ask each other the same question.

Notes: 1 This activity can be used to teach or revise the present continuous tense, and can usefully lead in to the past continuous tense, as illustrated below.
2 For teachers unsure of their drawing ability a number of drawings of people in action are given on page 111-113.

The past continuous tense: example 1

Characteristics and techniques: erasing information from the board.

If the board has been covered with drawings as in the example above, then write a name by each and erase them one by one asking a question each time. Leave just a little bit of each drawing as a reminder. The activity challenges the students' ability to remember all the different actions.

TEACHER: *(having erased one drawing)* What was Ron doing?
STUDENT: He was playing football.

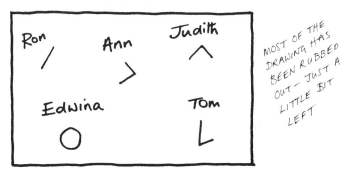

TEACHER:	*(having erased another drawing)* What was Ann doing?
STUDENT:	She was jumping.
TEACHER:	*(having erased another drawing)* What were Ron, Ann and Tom doing?
STUDENT:	Ron was playing football. Ann was jumping. Tom was diving.

The past continuous tense: example 2

Characteristics and techniques: a setting can be drawn on the board and large magazine pictures (publicity pictures, etc.) can be stuck on the picture in appropriate positions.

The build-up of the picture should be done through discussion with the class. Use the present continuous to discuss the actions as they are seen. Then remove the pictures and challenge the students' memories: 'Who was here? What was he doing?'

The simple past tense: example 1

Characteristics and techniques: erasing and substituting information.

Draw (or ask a student to draw) a person on the board.

TEACHER:	This is Stan Ross. He is fat and bald and he is very rich. He's not very happy! *(Drawing 1)*

Erase everything except Stan's head and boots. *(Drawing 2)* Ask a student to replace the erased parts with new drawing.

TEACHER:	Stan used to be thin and he had a lot of curly hair. He was poor but he was really happy.

The student then redraws Stan. *(Drawing 3)*

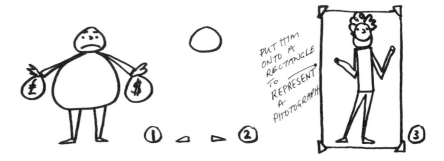

The simple past tense: example 2

Characteristics and techniques: erasing and substituting information.

Draw (or ask students to draw) a map of the district you and the students are familiar with. With the help of the students write on the map what the various shops are and any other information which you think important.

TEACHER/STUDENT: The shop on the corner is an electrician's. The next shop is a shoe repairer's.
etc.

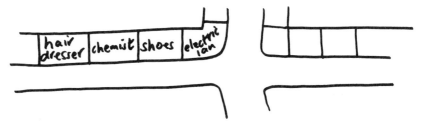

Discuss with the students their earliest memories of the district and change the map accordingly. Consider asking the students to ask their parents and grandparents what the district used to be like.

TEACHER/STUDENT: The shop on the corner used to be a clothes shop and the shop next door was a flower shop. The next shop was a chemist's.

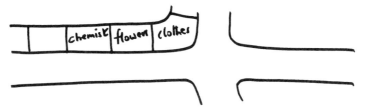

Used to

Characteristics and techniques: sticking pictures on the board and erasing and substituting information.

Stick six (or more) magazine pictures of people on the board. Join them with lines which show how they feel about each other.

likes ⟶

doesn't like ⟿

quite likes ⋯⋯⟩

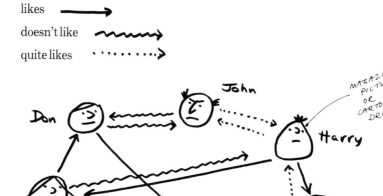

Ask such questions as:

TEACHER: Who does Sue like?
Who likes Bob?
Does John like Edwina?
Do John and Florence like each other?
Are Harry and Flo friends?

Erase and redraw some of the connecting lines and describe and ask questions about the relationships as they used to be.

TEACHER: Who did Sue use to like?
etc.

Note: Teachers and their students can invent a variety of characters who can then be referred to at any point as the need arises.

Prepositions

Characteristics and techniques: adding information and using coloured chalks.

Step one:
Draw (or ask students to draw) a map on the board.

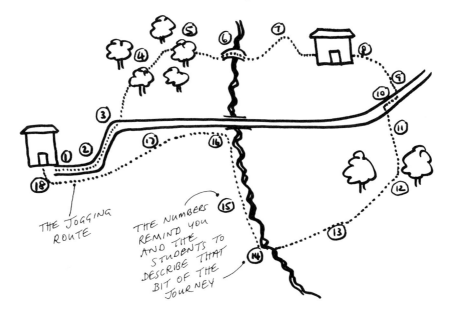

THE JOGGING ROUTE

THE NUMBERS REMIND YOU AND THE STUDENTS TO DESCRIBE THAT BIT OF THE JOURNEY

If the map is invented by the class then there is considerable opportunity for discussion and for the use of vocabulary to describe objects and locations.

Step two:
Say you are going to go jogging and then draw a route across the map with coloured chalk. Describe your route. If you place a number at each point you wish to identify, it will help you and the students to repeat what you have said. Ask the students to write down the route you took.
For example, they might write: 'You started outside your house. Then you ran down the road and around the first bend. At the second bend . . .'

Step three:
Using the range of verbs, prepositions and nouns you made use of (asking for others as required) each student makes a copy of the map or draws a new one and works out his or her own jogging route. Individual students describe their routes so that other students can draw the described route on the board with coloured chalk.

Sentence pattern table

Characteristics and techniques: information easy for the whole class to see can be added, pictures can be stuck on.

Draw a sentence pattern table on the board. (For hints on writing and designing see pages 100-108.)
Substitutions can be cued by words added to the columns or by holding up pictures, pointing to parts of a big picture or by sticking small pictures into the column.

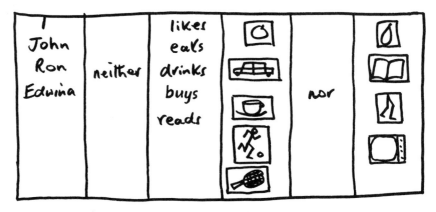

Notes: 1 This kind of practice is more mechanical than meaningful. A creative element can be introduced by encouraging the students to propose any words they like providing the sentence remains grammatically correct. In seeing that a suggestion is ridiculous and laughing about it the students experience the meaning of the language used.
2 A set of characters invented by the class and referred to constantly also adds interest and meaning even in the dullest of exercises. In this case Ron could be renowned as a crazy spendthrift once he goes shopping.

Questionnaires

Characteristics and techniques: building up information which all the class can see.

Grids can easily be drawn on the board and the spaces in the grid can be drawn in, written in or given ticks, etc. as a result of discussion. In the act of completing the grid, controlled language practice can take place. For example, in order to carry out the survey and complete the grid below, basic questions about liking and disliking must be asked and answered by each member of the class.

TEACHER: Do you like oranges?

STUDENT: Yes, a lot./No, not very much./No, not at all.

	oranges	apples	bananas
a lot	///////	//	////
not very much	/	///	///
not at all	/	//	/////////

Note: The formation and completion of this grid has a meaningful purpose. It might be interesting to find out which is the most popular and the least popular fruit (hobby/TV programme/sport/type of holiday). Grids of information can be drawn on the board which provide simple cues for answers to questions or for substitutions in sentences or for the gap completion of sentences.

Questions and answers

Characteristics and techniques: preparing the text before the lesson and covering part of the board with a cloth or large piece of paper.

Write a series of questions on the board before the lesson begins. Include the answers but in a separate column. Pin a cloth or piece of paper over the answers. The questions can be answered in writing by each individual and then discussed with a neighbour. Finally two pairs can work together until each group has an agreed set of answers. These answers can then be offered and discussed by the whole class. Finally the cloth can be removed and the correct answers revealed.

A CLOTH OR SHEET OF PAPER COVERING THE ANSWERS

PINS

Which is the largest animal?
Which is the highest mountain?
Which is the deepest ocean?
Which is the longest river?

Dialogue, role play and drama

Dialogue writing and acting

Characteristics and techniques: erasing and substituting information.

Write a dialogue on the board.

At the office
A: Hi, Bill!
B: Hi!
A: How's it going?
B: Not so good.
A: What's wrong?
B: Oh, you know how it is. A huge pile of work.

In the example below, students have, with the teacher's help, created an alternative dialogue based on the first dialogue given by the teacher. The information exchanged is broadly the same but the way in which the two people are speaking to each other is very different. In the first dialogue the two people are on familiar terms. In the second dialogue the people are on more formal terms. In order to bring out fully this change in the formality of the relationship, the two dialogues should be acted out.

At the office:

C: Good morning, Bill!
B: Oh, good morning, Mr Cavendish.
C: And how is the work progressing?
B: I'm afraid there are a few difficulties.
C: With respect Bill, if there were no difficulties there would be no job to do!

Dialogue with a single voice!

Characteristics and techniques: large simple pictures are easy to draw on the board. (For teachers unsure of their drawing ability see pages 108-116.)

Quite often the teacher wants to present a dialogue and to act out the part of two (or more) people. It is helpful both to the teacher and to the class if there are two large faces sketched on the board. The teacher can then point to the faces as he or she speaks their lines or even stand in front of them.

Drama

Characteristics and techniques: large sketches are quick to do and to adapt.

A scene can be sketched on the board by the teacher or by the students in a few minutes. The action of discussing what should be drawn and the drawing itself help to develop a sense of the context of the drama which is to be acted out. In the example below, two of the characters invented by the class might be waiting at a bus stop. The students, working in pairs, must imagine a dramatic episode and dialogue and act it out in front of the board 'theatre'.

Notes: 1 For tips on drawing see pages 108-116.
      2 For more ideas on role play and dialogue practice see pages 72-76. It would be advisable to introduce many of the ideas on the board before asking the students to work with role play cards.

Guided writing: adapting a story

Characteristics and techniques: erasing and substituting information.

Write the beginning of a short story on the board.

Last week Ron went to see his girlfriend in Stockport. He set off in his car at about seven o'clock. It was a cold winter's evening and he looked forward to a nice warm dinner. When he got to the house he saw that the windows were dark. The door was open. He went in and found...

Discuss it with the students. Ask the students for suggestions for how the story might be changed without adding significantly more words. One or several words can be added, erased or substituted. The example below shows the first few lines of the story in its second version, altered by the students.

Yesterday Edwina went to visit her Grandma at about five o'clock. It was a warm Summer's afternoon ....

Webs

Characteristics and techniques: developing diagrams which everyone can see through close discussion.

The use of webs in language teaching has flowered in recent years. (They are sometimes known as mind maps or word trees.) Only a few examples can be given in this book but the potential of webs should not be underestimated. Webs encourage students to see and to express a variety of relationships. The process of making the web is more important than the finished web. The act of making a web helps students to appreciate the meaning of the words involved and to remember them; for this reason the teacher should normally not dominate nor determine exactly how the web is made. Teachers can demonstrate the use of the web on the blackboard and then encourage students to develop their own webs in their books.

There are two broad divisions of webs: objective and subjective. In objective webs the grouping and relationship of the words can be justified by reference to common experience. In subjective webs the grouping and relationship of the words is justified primarily by the individual referring to his or her personal experiences.

Vocabulary webs

Characteristics and techniques: sticking a picture on the board, adding and erasing information.

Stick a picture on the board (or ask a student to draw a picture). Ask other students to come to the board and write down any words they associate with the picture. Add words yourself if you wish to enlarge the vocabulary of the class. In the first example, the teacher has developed a web with the class which arranges all the words they know under a general heading. In the second example, a student has written down his or her own associations with the starting word.

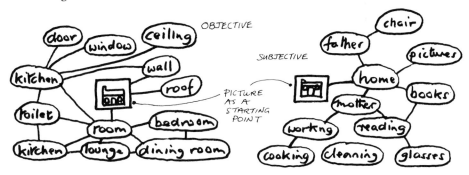

Note: This activity can also be done by individual students, in their vocabulary books, for example.

Story planning web

It is a common experience for teachers that the students find it difficult to talk about their experiences or to invent stories. And this is not surprising! In the example below the teacher has asked the students to develop their own web of experiences based on their last holiday. The example shows an individual student's web.

The form of the web has encouraged the student to relax so that each bit of information triggers off another bit of information. The next step is for the student to check whether or not he or she has the language to talk about these experiences. Key phrases can be written against each 'bubble'. One has been written in as an example. The student must use a dictionary, grammar book and/or the teacher to become equipped to talk about some of the points in the

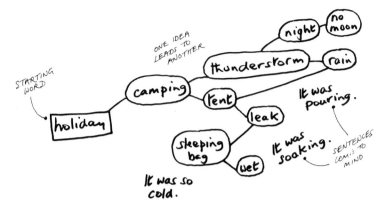

web. The final step is for the student to talk about or to write about his or her 'story'.

Open communicative practice

Pictures for speculation

Characteristics and techniques: building up a picture on the board through discussion with the class.

An ambiguous picture can be a stimulus for speculation and subsequently for dialogue work, for discussion of general themes, and for the rather specialised discussion of how the picture can be made less ambiguous. Each of these areas of focus and language is described below.

Draw an ambiguous picture on the board. It should be possible to interpret the picture in a variety of ways. It is important that you yourself should not have a fixed view of what the picture 'really' represents. The secret of inventing an ambiguous picture is to draw as little information as possible.

Speculation
Step one:
Ask the students to describe what they see. Very quickly the class will realise that some things are interpreted in a similar way (two people, a chair and a table) and other things are interpreted differently (outside or inside/home or school/people related or not).

Step two:
Encourage the 'opinion gap' between the students. Do not let them think that you have a fixed idea or that your interpretation is the correct one. When the opinion gaps have become apparent ask the students to note down what they

think the picture represents. (Accuracy is not as important as fluency at this stage.)

Step three:
Ask the students to work with their neighbour comparing interpretations. At this point students can change their opinions.

Step four:
Invite class discussion again. Encourage argument. For example:
STUDENT A: It can't be outside because tables and chairs are not outside.
STUDENT B: Chairs and tables can be outside – for example, in a café.

Making the picture less ambiguous
This activity contextualises the use of 'should', 'could', 'would'. The example below clearly illustrates that a simple drawing activity on the board can be used to give demanding language work for proficient speakers of the language.

Choose one of the interpretations being put forward and ask the students what you should have included in the drawing to make it clear. Here is an example of a conversation which might take place:

TEACHER: If I had wanted to show a classroom what should I have drawn?
STUDENT A: You should have drawn a lot of desks.
TEACHER: That's a good idea. But it would have been difficult because there isn't much space. So what should I have done?
STUDENT A: You could have drawn part of another desk.
TEACHER: Yes, I could have done that. But would it have been clearly a class?
STUDENT B: No, it could have been a café with lots of tables.
TEACHER: So, what should I have drawn?
STUDENT C: You should have written some maths on the blackboard.
TEACHER: Yes, that's a good idea. If I had written some maths on the rectangle at the top it would have looked like a blackboard. So the room would have looked like a classroom. If I had wanted to show that the teacher is a woman what should I have drawn?
STUDENT D: You should have drawn long hair and a skirt.
TEACHER: Yes, good idea!

(You draw in the extra information once you have negotiated it with the students.)

Personal experiences and discussion of a general theme
Take a theme which has developed in the discussion and ask students to contribute their personal experiences and opinions. For example, the picture may have been interpreted and developed as representing a quarrel.

Students can talk about: disagreements and quarrels they have had; their attitude to differences of opinion; the different ways that people in different circumstances express their differences of opinion (or not).

Dialogue

Having agreed on what is happening in the picture, speculate on what may have happened just before the incident in the picture and what might happen next. Ask the students to invent dialogues which take place before, during and after the time in the picture.

Follow-up activities

Any of the above activities can be continued into pair and groupwork on paper.

Picture sequence story

Characteristics and techniques: developing a series of drawings through discussion with the class.

Draw (or ask a student to draw) a picture of a person or an object on the board. The drawing should be towards the left hand side of the board in case it proves to be the first in a sequence of drawings.

Ask the students to suggest the beginning of a story. Encourage and welcome any suggestions and avoid correcting grammatical mistakes at this point. Through discussion with the class, agree on one of the proposals (or a combination of the proposals). Ask another student to draw either some more information to go with the first picture or to begin a new picture. Invite ideas for how the story might continue incorporating the new drawing. Here is an example:

1 There was a big black box.
2 It was under a tree.
3 A cloud came and it began to rain.
4 A man sat on the box under the tree. He didn't want to get wet.
5 Suddenly, the box began to move!
   etc.

Listening

Characteristics and techniques: drawing pictures and writing on the board.

Key words and sentences, together with pictures and maps can be used to prepare students before they listen to a description or to a story. The students can begin to predict what the text might be about by looking at the key words and pictures on the board.

In this use of words and pictures on the board, the preparation can be done before the class enters the room.

Here are four basic types of text for listening:

Description of a place

Description of a scene and of people and objects

Description of an incident, a process or a story

A dialogue
In this case the teacher (or students) point to the person who is speaking or to the object referred to.

Grammatical explanation

Characteristics and techniques: adding and highlighting information with coloured chalks.

Text analysis

The features of a text can be highlighted and relationships between parts of a text can be demonstrated by underlining, encircling and by using coloured chalks.

John bought a car as soon as (he) could afford (it).

Full and reduced sentences

Characteristics and techniques: erasing.

The chalkboard helps you to show the relationship between full and reduced sentences.

That is the one which I ate.
That's the one   I ate.

letters and words rubbed out

Tense

Characteristics and techniques: adding and highlighting information with coloured chalk.

You can use a picture and a series of lines to help students to appreciate aspects of the meaning of a tense form.

In this example, a simple drawing of a man running and a house imply that the man has just left the house and begun his run. In the second drawing he looks exhausted but he is still running. This implies that it is later on. The diagrammatic line offers another way of generalising about the use of the structure. The advantage of the chalkboard over a wallchart of the same drawing and diagram is that the students can see the 'story' develop and see the analytic diagram related to the drawing sequence.

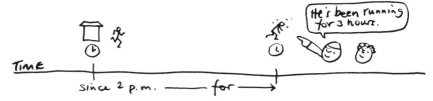

Vocabulary grouping

Characteristics and techniques: several people can work together at the board at the same time and coloured chalks can be used.

Some teachers believe it is important to help the students to develop their ability to find useful generalisations about the language for themselves. In the following example the students are being encouraged to 1 search for generalisations 2 evaluate the usefulness of the generalisations they discover.

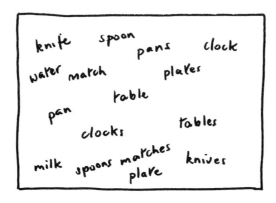

Step one:
Ask the students to call out all the words they can remember which are associated with a particular topic (or with a picture they are shown). Ask two or three students to act as secretaries and to write down all the words which are called out.
This activity can be done as a competition or challenge. The class can see how many words they can compile on the board in a fixed amount of time.

Step two:
Ask the students to write down in their books all the words on the board and then to think of as many different ways of grouping them as possible. Tell the students that no grouping can be wrong and that you are interested in them collecting as many as possible.
For example: by numbers of letters in the word; by grammar; by rarity; by whether they can be eaten or not!
After ten minutes, tell the students to work with their neighbour and compile a list in common.
Possibly then ask pairs to work with other pairs

Step three:
Students call out their ideas for grouping the words and these are discussed according to why they were chosen and then at a second stage how useful such groupings might be.

In the example given above, singular and plural forms might be scattered randomly on the board. The teacher then asks the students to suggest various ways of grouping the words according to the evidence on the board. A variety of groupings will be suggested. The teacher encourages the students and does not at this stage behave negatively to any of the suggestions. The generalisations are discussed. Before focusing on singular and plural forms, the teacher could then give the students a text in which there are examples of singular and plural forms in context. The students can then try out their theories to see if they seem to apply to the text. Finally the students can be asked for their observations on what generalisations they can find for the formation of the plural in English. Similar-coloured chalk can be used to rewrite the endings of words following the same generalisation, for example, knife/knives, leaf/ leaves. Other ways of using coloured chalks include: spelling, sound/spelling relationships, agreements.

Technical tips

1 The lighter-coloured chalks, white and yellow show more clearly on the chalkboard than the darker colours, red and blue.
2 Write letters and draw picture details big enough to be seen the length of

the classroom. Letters should be about 3 cm in height, clearly formed and contrasting in colour with the background if they are to be read easily from about 10 m away. However, it is best to check by asking the students at the back of the class.

3 Usually keep lines of text horizontal. You can rule lines on the whiteboard with a permanent marker pen in a slightly darker colour than the surface of the board. A grid of horizontal and vertical lines just visible to you but not obtrusive to the class is most useful for keeping a discipline for your writing and for helping you to draw rapidly.

4 Use the side of the chalk as an alternative to the pointed end. This will give you, without effort, a variety of lines which are useful in underlining, in drawing boxes, and in drawing.

5 For tips on design, drawing and lettering (see pages 100-116).
6 Don't stand with your back to the class for too long!
7 Don't obscure your writing with your body or arm.
8 Clean the board from top to bottom and preferably with a wet cloth to reduce the dust.
9 Repaint the chalkboard when necessary.
10 Utilise the shelf at the bottom of the board for picture or word cards. (If there isn't one then ask for one!)

11 Add a wire across the top of the chalkboard plus clips for
   (a) pictures
   (b) sheets of text
   (c) word cards making sentences
   (d) sheets covering part of the board, for example, hiding questions to answers or for use as a projection screen.

12 Use the board beneath the pictures suspended on the wire to make comments. On a whiteboard it is easier to stick a picture on the surface and then write comments on the whiteboard around it.
13 Sticking pictures on an unmagnetised board is not easy! Blu-Tack (or similar plastic adhesive) is affected by chalk dust. Make sure that you clean the chalkboard well where you want to stick it and knead it well before use.
   A dab of latex glue is effective and does not mark the board when dry.

2 Overhead projector

There are overhead projectors in many schools and colleges but not always in the hands of language teachers. This is a pity because they are one of the most useful tools a language teacher can have. The teacher can use the transparencies again and again and, at the same time, can adapt and create images of many kinds.

Characteristics and techniques

1 The whole class can see the projected image.
2 The image can be projected without darkening the room.
3 Text and pictures can be modified in front of the class:
   - adding a transparency or taking one away;
   - writing on the transparency or wiping lines off;
   - obscuring or revealing parts of the transparency by putting something opaque on the screen or removing it, for example, a book.
4 Transparencies can be prepared beforehand and used many times.
5 Permanent pens make transparencies which last for a long time; the marks of water-based pens can be removed with a damp cloth.
6 There are pens with a variety of thicknesses of nib and in a variety of colours.
7 Transparencies can be made by photocopying.

As the techniques associated with an overhead projector (OHP) are so distinctive, activities will be described under technique headings.

Single unprepared transparency

Characteristics and techniques: you or the students can write or draw directly on the transparency as you would on the chalkboard but with the advantages of projected size, brightness of colour and clarity. Thus most of the activities described under chalkboard in the previous section could be done on the OHP.

Describing pictures: example 1

Draw parts of a picture and ask the students to guess what is happening.

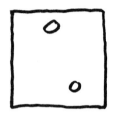

TEACHER: Tell me about the picture.
STUDENT A: It's a man. That's his head.
STUDENT B: He's playing football. That's the ball.

Describing pictures: example 2

Draw a picture of something or someone. Ask the students to describe it. Then add some other features to the drawing and contradict the student (teasingly!) and ask the students to tell you again what is happening. The students can take over your role once they have got the idea.

TEACHER: *(having drawn the first stage of the picture)* Tell me about the picture.
STUDENT A: It's a man.
TEACHER: What's he doing?
STUDENT A: He's standing.
TEACHER: *(adding a skirt and long hair)* No, it isn't a man! Tell me about the picture.
STUDENT B: It's a woman.
TEACHER: What's she doing?
STUDENT B: She's standing.
TEACHER: *(changing the legs to running)* No, she isn't! What's she doing? etc.

Single prepared transparency

Characteristics and technniques: one of the basic advantages of the OHP is that you can prepare a text or a picture and use it instantly and as often as you wish without further work. Ideas for using texts and pictures are given throughout this book and many apply to the OHP. For that reason we have chosen some less usual examples which exploit the special characteristics of the OHP.

Reading

Put a text on the projector back to front and challenge the class to read it!

Sentence construction

Put a number of strips of text on the projector and challenge the students to place them in a logical sequence.

Storytelling

Prepare a number of strips of transparency with a small drawing on each one, for example, a car, a man, a cat, etc. You and the students can then move these pictures on the screen and illustrate a story.

Single transparency with a water-based pen

Characteristics and techniques: usually the transparency is prepared before the class with a permanent pen. During the class the teacher or the students can add information with a water-based pen. The additions in water-based ink can be cleaned off at any time.

Cloze test

A cloze test can be written in permanent based pen and a water-based pen can be used in a joint class effort to complete it.

It was raining and the bus — late. Neville — at his watch again. But really there — no hurry. He — really care about the bus or the rain. There — more important things in his mind.

Correcting texts

An essay containing mistakes can be projected. The teacher and students can correct it using a water-based pen.

London is/capital city of Britain.
        the

Translation and text analysis

A text can be written in permanent pen with wide spaces between the lines. The spaces can then be used for a translation written in water-based ink. Alternatively, the spaces can be used to mark in stress and intonation.

Good morning! How are you?

Terrible! It's the worst day of my life.

Listening

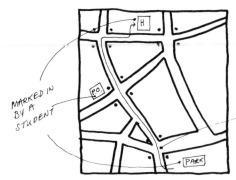

A map or street plan can be prepared in permanent pen. The teacher might read out a description of a journey taken across the city or might describe the location of various places on the map. A student can be asked to draw in the route or mark in the places with a water-based pen. Having understood the activity, all the students can then be asked to complete a similar plan instructed by the teacher or by another student.

Guided writing

A text can be prepared in water-based pen. During the lesson the class can discuss and make modifications to the text in which they might erase words and substitute others to see if they can change the sense without changing the grammar.

Everything was reassuring; the warm sunshine, the cheerful faces of the people in the park and above all the prospects which lay before him.

Elimination text

A text can be prepared in water-based pen. The class attempt to reduce the text to nothing. You allow them to remove one, two, or three adjacent words. They can change the meaning of the text but the grammar must remain correct. (A technique learnt from Mario Rinvolucri.)

The young red-haired woman crept quietly down the stairs.

REPLACE THE WORDS WITH LINES IF YOU WISH.

The ⸺ ⸺ ⸺ woman crept quietly down the stairs.
The ⸺ ⸺ ⸺ woman crept quietly ⸺ ⸺ ⸺.
The ⸺ ⸺ ⸺ woman ⸺ ⸺ ⸺ ⸺.

⸺ ⸺ ⸺ ⸺ ⸺ ⸺ ⸺.

Spelling and Scrabble

GRID IN PERMANENT PEN

A Scrabble grid can be prepared in permanent ink. The game can be played with letters added in water-based ink which can be cleaned off at the end of each game.

In one simple version of the game, the grid of squares is projected and the class try to fill it with as many words as possible, each word overlapping the others.

WORDS WRITTEN ON THE TRANSPARENCY IN WATER-BASED PEN WHICH CAN BE CLEANED OFF.

Note: For other spelling games see 'tic, tac, toe', 'noughts and crosses' and 'hangman'.

Two or more transparencies

Characteristics and techniques: you can add information or take it away by preparing several transparencies. Translations, annotations, additions and modifications can all be made by placing a second, third, (or more) transparency on the top of the first one.

Vocabulary

A picture can be projected and a second transparency added with words naming objects and actions.

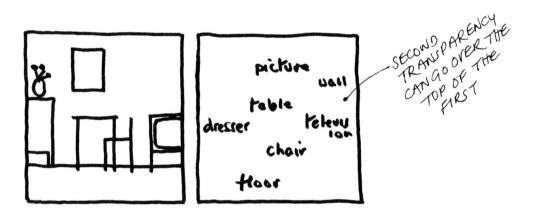

picture
wall
table
dresser
televus
ion
chair
floor

SECOND TRANSPARENCY CAN GO OVER THE TOP OF THE FIRST

Comparing differences

A picture can be projected (1), removed, and then substituted by another similar picture (2). The students try to remember and spot the differences between the two pictures. Then the two pictures are shown together (3). If a different colour is used for each drawing then the differences between the two pictures can be easily seen.

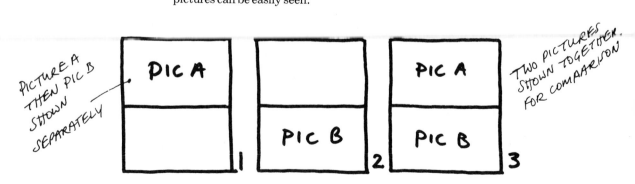

PICTURE A THEN PIC B SHOWN SEPARATELY

PIC A

PIC B

PIC A

PIC B

1

2

3

TWO PICTURES SHOWN TOGETHER. FOR COMPARISON

Identifying texts

Two texts can be laid one on top of the other. The students can be challenged to identify each text and to write each of them down.

Most eggs in Britain are brown.
Most American in the United States are
The North white in the animal
bear is a dangerous reason it has that the
particular, when think brown run the
British bear and the swim are
healthy, bear the Americans think
cubs. the quickly, it so think
that white, eggs healthy.
very
and climb trees
difficult to escape!

TWO TRANSPARENCIES
ONE OVER THE
OTHER

Masking and revealing

Characteristics and techniques: any opaque object can be laid on the projector and used to obscure what is beneath.

Learning a song

Put up a song on the OHP and mask it with something opaque. You can show one line at a time as the class learns it.

Predicting a text

You use a piece of paper or card to obscure the right hand half of a text. The students must guess at the missing parts. Instead of the right hand half, it could be the left or the bottom of the text.

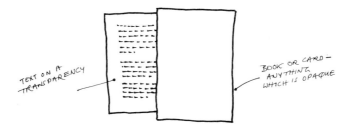

TEXT ON A TRANSPARENCY

BOOK OR CARD —
ANYTHING
WHICH IS OPAQUE

Discussion

You can place a text or a picture on the projector and hold a piece of card (a book or envelope) under the mirror which projects the image. This prevents any part of the image being projected. Move the card rapidly to and fro thus flashing the image on the screen. Ask the students what they saw. Get them to express their views and their differences of opinion. As them to write down what they saw and to discuss it with their neighbour. Flash the image again and once more prompt discussion and the expression of differences of perception and opinion.

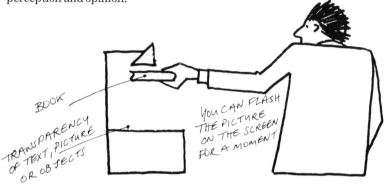

BOOK

TRANSPARENCY OF TEXT, PICTURE OR OBJECTS

YOU CAN FLASH THE PICTURE ON THE SCREEN FOR A MOMENT

Predictive reading

A piece of card or paper can have a hole cut in it. Place this on the projector and then pass a text slowly across it. If the hole is very small so that only one or two letters can be seen then the students are stimulated to guess at the word. As they establish a word so they are stimulated to guess at the next word making use of what they know about sentence construction, cohesion and collocation.

A picture or a picture strip can be shown and made use of in a similar way.

HOLE IN THE CARD

The p(io) was opened and the birds began to sing etc.

CARD

THE IMAGE PROJECTED ON THE SCREEN is BLACK EXCEPT FOR THE HOLE AND THE LETTERS PASSED ACROSS IT.

Vocabulary

Objects can be placed on the projector and their silhouettes projected on the screen. The students can be asked to guess what they are. If there are several objects then you can project them for a few moments and then cover the lens and ask the students to tell you what they saw and remember. You could remove one and then project the image again and ask them what you have done.

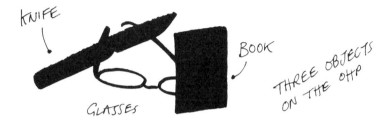

Expressive talking and writing

Anything can be laid on the projector! You can lay your head on it and project a profile image of yourself talking!
You can put a glass plate of water on the projector and arrange grasses around it and create a pond and a meadow! Try sliding a book, or better, your fingers slowly under the lens (careful, it might be hot!). This will create effects of sunrise, sunset and twilight! All these effects can be used to stimulate expressive talking and writing.

Drama and story-telling

Put the projector behind the screen (if it is a free standing screen) and you have a shadow puppet theatre! The students can make shadow puppets or use themselves as actors. Groups of students can be responsible for writing a play, making the props, acting it and telling the story.

Technical tips

1 Students at the back of the class must be able to see what you have written. Letters should be about 5mm high on the transparency if they are to be seen about 10 m away. Of course, the size of the image is partly dependent on how far away your projector is from the screen.

2 A few words and short sentences are best for the OHP. Handwriting (as on the chalkboard) should not be too idiosyncratic! Have full body shapes to the letters and minimise the length of the ascenders and descenders. For more tips on handwriting see pages 107 and 108.

3 Transparencies are made in different thicknesses and this affects the cost of them. Find which is suitable for you.

4 Yellow and orange do not project as well as red, blue and purple.

5 You might consider using a size of transparency which can be easily stored. We use A4 transparencies for this reason rather than the larger square shape.

6 Apart from writing and drawing on the transparency, you can also make transparencies from existing material by photocopying. Make sure however, that the text is big enough. Most texts in books are not big enough if reproduced on the transparency at the same size. Note, however, that many photocopying machines will enlarge the original. This will enable you to have a bigger letter size and satisfactory readability.

7 If your screen is not tilted (and it probably isn't) you may project a picture which is wider at the top than at the bottom. If this bothers you, then stick two strips of card down each side of the projector glass to correct this effect. You can also use these strips to narrow the image if you are using A4.

TWO STRIPS OF CARD TO CREATE A RECTANGLE ON THE OHP SCREEN

8 Check the OHP works before the lesson: make sure the bulb is working, that the OHP is in focus and that the lens is clean.

3 Flannelboard, magnetboard and adhesive plastic

All three media enable pictures or texts on paper or card to be displayed to the class.

Flannelboard: cutout figures (pictures or words) are backed by flannel, rough sandpaper or teazlestrip (e.g. Velcro) and are placed on a vertical board covered with flannel or blanket-like material.

Magnetboard: cutout figures have a small piece of strip magnet stuck on the back or placed on the front. The surface of the board is zinc or tinplate metal sheet. The figures adhere much better than on the flannelboard. On the other hand, the magnetboard is more inconvenient because it is much heavier and the magnets can be difficult to acquire and to keep.

Adhesive plastic: a plastic is widely available which can be torn into small pieces and moulded with the fingers into small balls. It can then be used to stick paper or card onto most smooth surfaces. In many ways this is the most useful of the three media if it is available to the teacher. One well-known version is called Blu-Tack.

ON MAGNETBOARD AND BOARDS USED FOR STICKING ADHESIVE PLASTIC BACKGROUND LINES CAN BE DRAWN

WORDCARDS AND PICTURES STUCK ON THE BACKGROUND THEY CAN BE MOVED ABOUT

Characteristics and techniques

All three media:

1 All three media are essentially for use by the teacher and material displayed should be big enough for the whole class to see.
2 Sentences and scenes can 'grow' or diminish in front of the class as words or pictures are added, moved or taken away.
3 The words and pictures can be handled by the teacher or students before being placed on the board or surface.
4 On the magnetboard, background settings (for example, a street) can be drawn on large pieces of paper and placed on the board. Pictures of objects and people can be placed on top of this background setting. Pictures can be placed on top of other pictures.
5 With adhesive plastic no preparation is required and any piece of paper or card can be stuck or moved from one position to another. Pictures can be placed on top of other pictures including large pieces of paper representing settings.
6 Essentially all three media allow the teacher and students to simulate in a very simple form and with great flexibility, scenes, situations and stories as well as diagrams and short texts. Thus a great variety of language can be contextualised through the use of these media.
7 Teachers nervous of drawing on the chalkboard can prepare visuals in advance with these three media.

Presentation and controlled practice

Characteristics and techniques: showing one or more pictures illustrating objects or actions.

At the most basic level, pictures can be used to introduce the meaning of language new to the students or to cue answers to questions or substitutions within sentences.

Presenting vocabulary

TEACHER: This is a cat. It's on the table! Now it's under the table!
etc.

Vocabulary practice

The teacher puts a large piece of paper on the board (magnetboard only) with the outline of an elephant drawn on it. He or she then places food inside the elephant. Students take it in turns to name the food and then to list all the other food the elephant has eaten.

TEACHER: What's this?
STUDENT: It's an apple.
TEACHER: So, what has the elephant eaten?
STUDENT: The elephant has eaten a piece of cake, a cabbage, some sugar and an apple.
etc.

Open communicative practice

Characteristics and techniques: the flexibility of being able to give students pictures to hold which they can then come to the front of the class and stick on the board.

The students can be divided into pairs or groups. Each student can be given one picture and/or word and students take it in turns to place their pictures on the board. They must be able to say what connection their picture has with the last picture or word placed there. If the class like the idea, the picture can be left on the board.

The activity can be done by having only two pictures which have to be related or by telling a story with each successive picture illustrating the next part of the story.

In this example, the two pictures have been related:

STUDENT: The ghost has lived in this house for three hundred years.

Listening comprehension and oral retelling

Characteristics and techniques: building up a situation, moving pictures to illustrate a story.

These three media lend themselves to the established audio visual approach of using pictures to illustrate a story or a dialogue. The understanding of the story helps the student to understand the meaning of language new to them. The students having heard and understood the story then retell it, act out the dialogue and change the pictures as required.

Owing to shortage of space in this book, only three scenes of the story are illustrated below. However, in the classroom the number of intermediary stages is limited only by the number of pictures the teacher can get hold of.

When Ron was a baby he used to be so nice and so happy. He used to play with his teddy bear. And everybody used to like him . . .
etc.

When Ron was twenty he was a student. He was poor but he was happy. He used to live in a little room and in the winter he used to wear his coat in his room because he hadn't got enough money for a heater. He didn't play with his teddy bear anymore but he used to keep it with him for luck!
etc.

(Note: the picture of Ron at twenty can be stuck on top of the picture of Ron as a baby.)

Now he is fifty. He has a car and a big house but he is a miserable man. He is always complaining. No one likes him.

The first few developments in a story are illustrated here. The picture grows and changes according to the stage in the story.

Technical tips

Magnetboard

1 Magnetboards can be made easily and cheaply. Hardware shops sell the metal plate. Check that magnets stick to it. The metal should be about 1 m by 1.5 m depending on how you can cope with the weight. The metal should be mounted on a wooden frame or against a wooden board. The alternative is to use a metal cupboard if there is one convenient. (As mentioned before, some whiteboards are already magnetised.)
2 Magnetic strip can be obtained from refrigerator repairers; it is used as the seal on refrigerator doors. Hardware shops or stationers sometimes sell magnetic strips or small, flat magnets.

Flannelboard

1 Flannel or blanket-like material should be stretched on a board. Because the figures do not adhere as well as on a magnetboard it is an advantage to position the board so that it is leaning rather than vertical.
2 The figures must have a rough surface on the back which adheres to the board. Sandpaper or flannel itself will work reasonably well. However, a commercial product like flock paper or teazel or Velcro is better.

Adhesive plastic

The surface should be free from dust. The chalkboard ought to be sponged clean and must be allowed to dry before the adhesive will stick. An alternative is a rubber glue which peels off when dry and does not damage the surface or the picture.

Notes for all three media

1 Pictures can be cut from magazines. Very often it is more satisfactory to draw them and to colour them with felt tip pens.
2 Some teachers do not attempt to have individual pictures for all objects. They have a number of symmetrical shapes which they introduce at the beginning of each activity as symbols of particular objects. Here are examples of the sort of basic shapes which can be used to symbolise different things:

The advantage of this approach is not only that it is time saving but that some students like the challenge to their imagination.
3 In all cases it is advisable to mount the pictures on thin card and to cover them with a clear, self-adhesive plastic so that they can be used many times.

4 Wallpictures and wallposters

Wallpictures and wallposters illustrate scenes, people or objects and are large enough to be seen by all the students.
Wallpictures may be:

1 produced commercially for language teaching purposes (see Byrne, D and Hall, D, 1976 *Wall Pictures for Language Practice* Longman);
2 produced for other educational purposes, for example, a road safety poster, or for commercial purposes unconnected with education, for example, a publicity poster;
3 produced by the teacher and/or students, either drawn or made by collage (see page 116).

MAGAZINE PHOTOGRAPHS CUT OUT AND STUCK ON A LARGE SHEET OF PAPER

SIMPLE DRAWING. FOR TIPS ON DRAWING SEE PAGES 108-116

Characteristics and techniques

1 Wallpictures often show a complicated scene and contain many details. If the students cannot see the necessary detail or if they are distracted by the rest of the picture then that is clearly a disadvantage. On the other hand, it is the very complexity of most wallpictures which makes some activities so useful.
2 The whole class can see the picture.
3 It is ready to use and can be used more than once.
4 It can be left on display or taken down.

Presentation and guided practice

Characteristics and techniques: a wallpicture like the one illustrated above provides a context for language use and a variety of reference for controlled practice in both speaking and writing.

Wallpictures have a traditional role in the presenting of new language, both vocabulary and structures, to the students. In the hand-drawn picture illustrated above, the teacher can introduce many words for people and objects seen in a street. The scene as a whole gives a context for this new language and an opportunity to move into controlled practice by the students.

The present perfect tense

Traditionally, the wallpicture is associated with the present continuous tense. However, other tense forms can be introduced and practised, for example, the present perfect:

TEACHER: *(pointing at the man coming out of the shop)* This man is coming out of the shop. He's got a bag. He's bought something. What has he bought, do you think?
And this woman, she's dropped something on the pavement. What has she dropped?

Having introduced the present perfect, the teacher might write a sentence pattern table on the board and ask the students to offer more examples based on the picture. For example:

STUDENT A: The cat has climbed the tree.
STUDENT B: The plane has left the airport.
STUDENT C: The woman has crossed the road.

Might

Scenes always imply that something has happened before the time in the picture and that something is going to happen afterwards. The teacher can exploit this. For example:

TEACHER: What might the woman have done before her bag broke?
STUDENT A: She might have put too many heavy things in it.
TEACHER: What might she do next?
STUDENT B: She might wrap the shopping in her scarf.

True/false game

Controlled practice does not always need to be an occasion when the students merely articulate the language. Activities can be introduced which make the student think about meaning and want to communicate it. For example, the well-known true/false game can be used. The teacher (or a student) makes a number of statements some of which are true and some of which are false. If this is done orally then the students can correct the teacher when he or she makes a false statement. For example:

TEACHER: The cat is being chased by the dog.
STUDENTS: No! The dog is being chased by the cat!
(In the picture, the dog really is being chased by the cat!)

If the true/false game is done in writing, then the teacher might write a number of sentences on the board and ask the students to copy the correct ones and to correct and then copy the incorrect ones.

Once this version of the activity has been done, each student can write a number of sentences making some true and some false. The students then read out each other's sentences if they are true.

Memory game

Another well-established game which can transform a mechanical exercise into real communication is the memory game. The teacher stands with his or her back to the picture and tries to describe everything in it. The students correct the teacher whenever he or she makes a mistake, a source of great satisfaction to the students. Once the students have understood the game they can try it out in pairs or groups for themselves with one of them (or possibly two) trying to describe the picture from memory.

Hide and seek

Prepositions can be practised with the game of 'hide and seek'. One student imagines that he or she is a mouse and is hiding somewhere in the picture. The other students try to find out where the mouse is hiding.

STUDENT A:	Are you in the old man's pocket?
STUDENT MOUSE:	No.
STUDENT B:	Are you behind the tree in the park?
STUDENT MOUSE:	No.
	etc.

Older students might prefer to imagine that they have hidden something in the picture.

Guided writing

You can give the students a text with some words or sentences missing. The students complete the text by referring to the picture.

Dialogues

Characteristics and techniques: the quantity and variety of information related to a theme in both wallpictures on page 44 provides a context for dialogue and role play.

The dialogues can be controlled as in the first example below or open as in the second example.

Controlled dialogue

Write a model dialogue on the board which one or two pairs of students act out in front of the class. When you feel that all the students understand the dialogue, ask them to work with a neighbour and to devise a new dialogue substituting other words for those which are underlined, based on the picture. Your dialogue might be like this:

SMALL BOY: Where are we going now, <u>Mummy</u>?
MOTHER: We are going to <u>the baker's</u>.

Students might change the dialogue to:

CAT: Where are we going now, Fred?
DOG: We are going to the park.

Open dialogue

In this example, students have studied the wallpicture of animals on page 44 and have invented and written a dialogue which they can then act out for the class or direct another pair to act for them. The students have used the pictures of animals on the poster as a reference rather than as a setting for their dialogue.

ANIMAL RIGHTS WOMAN:	You shouldn't kill birds.
HUNTER:	Why not?
ANIMAL RIGHTS WOMAN:	Because it is wrong.
HUNTER:	But the birds eat the corn.
ANIMAL RIGHTS WOMAN:	These birds don't eat corn, they eat insects.

Vocabulary

Characteristics and techniques: the picture can be displayed quickly and its complexity can provide a rich source of vocabulary practice.

The students call out in, say, five minutes all the words they remember which can be related to the picture. More advanced students can be restricted to certain kinds of word, for example, adjectives. One or two student 'secretaries' write down all the words given by the class on the board.
As the students call out the words you should make a rapid note of them. (Alternatively be ready to cover the board with paper or a cloth.)

When all the words have been written down, give the students a moment to look at them and then erase them. Each student then tries to remember all the words and to write them down. After five minutes ask the students to work with their neighbour and to compile a joint list. After another five minutes ask pairs of students to work together in groups of four to compile their final composite list. Tell the students to put their words into alphabetical order. See which group remembers the most words.

Listening comprehension

Characteristics and techniques: the variety and complexity of information in the wallpicture mean that students must listen or read very carefully in order to identify what is being referred to.

The teacher describes. 1 a person's appearance in the picture
2 a person's thoughts   3 an object   4 what the teacher thinks about anything in the picture. The students try to say who or what is being described. The description can be easy both conceptually and linguistically or be very demanding in both senses. Here is a description intended for beginners:

TEACHER:	He is thinking. 'I must go slowly. It's dangerous.'
STUDENT A:	The man on the motorbike.
TEACHER:	Yes.

A more demanding example:

TEACHER: What a wonderful quiet place to retreat to in the lunch break.
STUDENT B: The park.
TEACHER: Yes.

Free communicative practice

Characteristics and techniques: the variety and complexity of information offers considerable choice of what to talk about.

Speculation

With the wallpicture made of magazine pictures of animals (page 44), the students could be asked to identify the animals, to say where they live and to talk about their characteristics. The students can then be asked to discuss broader issues such as, 'the relationship between these animals and people', 'animal rights', 'animals in history', and their own personal associations with these animals.

Story-telling

In the picture of the street scene (page 44) there is a great variety of information which could provide a basis for story-telling. Students might be asked to imagine what one of the people is thinking or feeling and to write a short story about him or her. The story could include reference to several places or other people in the picture.

Technical tips

1 The students at the back of the class must be able to see and recognise the details that you want them to see. The only way to ensure this happens is to test it. As a general rule details must be about 2 cm in height to be seen the length of the classroom. Nevertheless, testing is the only way of being sure.
2 Teachers and students can make wallpictures by drawing them and/or by sticking pictures from magazines, etc. on to the paper. Although the result is, by definition, amateurish the students are very likely to appreciate it as much or more than a commercially produced picture.
3 The drawing style used must be almost diagrammatic with clear, simple outlines and simple colour-filled shapes rather than a sketchy, impressionistic style which is difficult to 'read'.
4 The easiest way to store wallpictures is to fold them neatly, unless you have access to a map rack or shelf.
5 For more suggestions for drawing, mounting and displaying wallpictures see pages 108 to 118.

5 Picture flash cards

Picture flash cards are pictures mounted or drawn on cards approximately 15 cm by 20 cm. They are normally used by the teacher in oral work for cueing responses to questions or in more open communicative work for stimulating conversation, story-telling, etc. The normal picture card has a picture on one side only. However, both sides can be used and the card can be folded or cut in various ways with particular teaching purposes in mind.

Characteristics and techniques

1 Picture cards are easy and inexpensive for the teacher to prepare which means that sets of cards related to language teaching points or to subject matter can be built up over a period of time.
2 The cards are easy to store and to carry to the classroom so they offer considerable flexibility to the teacher in the conduct of the lesson.
3 The cards can be shown to the whole class or to a single student which allows the teacher to control who receives the information on them.
4 Because they are held and can be presented at speed or in a leisurely manner, the teacher can control the pace, variety and interest of the lesson.
5 The teacher can show one or two cards at any one time by hand. However, the cards can also be propped on a shelf, for example, at the bottom of the

chalkboard. The cards can also be pinned on a board, or stuck to a magnetboard or to any smooth surface with adhesive plastic. The student can be asked to stand at the front of the class and to hold cards. In this way a great number of cards can be displayed.

6 The cards can be used in groupwork by the students.

Presentation

Characteristics and techniques: there is great flexibility in being able to show one or several picture cards at key moments.

Teaching meaning with one picture

Sometimes it is possible to show a single picture illustrating a new word and expect it to be understood. For example, a bicycle:

Teaching meaning using several pictures

Usually it is advisable to show several pictures to be sure that the students know what you are referring to. For example, in teaching the present perfect continuous: He's been swimming. She's been climbing. They've been eating. These cards can be shown to the class and then propped on a shelf, each reinforcing the others.

Contrasting meanings

Sometimes it is helpful to introduce contrasting language items at the same time. The two pictures can be placed on either side of the card. In the act of turning the card over the contrast is demonstrated. The examples given below are: can/can't, likes/doesn't like, too big/too small:

Comparing meanings

Card can also be folded. In the example below, the difference between 'hill' and 'mountain' is demonstrated. Each one may be seen by itself or in comparison with the other.

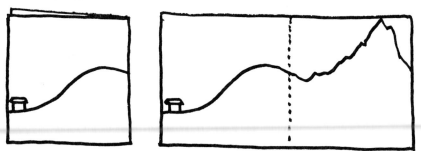

Presenting meanings of new words in a story

Sometimes it is essential to introduce the new language within a longer text, perhaps a story. The language which is already known to the student leads to an understanding of the story and this understanding of the story indicates the meaning of the new language. Picture cards can be used to illustrate the story and by making the story more readily understood, the new language, in turn, might be understood by the student. It is important to say 'might be' because it is often difficult to ascertain just how people have responded to and interpreted the information they have received.

Folding card story

A miniature story is created simply by folding the paper. By folding the paper into three panels, three stages in the story can be illustrated and this, in turn, illustrates three tense forms.

He's going to sit on the cat.
He's sitting on the cat.
He has sat on the cat.

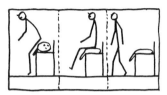 

Note: If you show one example of this three fold story, you could ask the students to produce one of their own for homework. Although it would only involve them in dealing with one example of these three tense forms, it would nevertheless be very intensive and memorable. They would also be able to show their work to their fellow students and more practice would occur.

Practice

Characteristics and techniques: a great variety of pictures can be shown at a moment's notice to the students one after the other or the cards can be placed on a shelf. The pictures can provide reference for the students as they answer or ask questions, make substitutions or complete sentences.

TEACHER: *(holding up a picture of some apples)* I've been to the shops. What did I buy?
STUDENT: You bought some apples.

Alternatively, don't show the picture to the students, so that they must guess what you have bought. The language practice is the same but the interest is greater and the language is used more meaningfully.

Pictures and sentence patterns

The teacher might wish to write a sentence model table on the board to guide the students and then use picture flash cards to cue variations. Usually this kind of work requires the student to think very little about the meaning of what he or she is saying. It is possible, however, to plan the activity so that the student must give more thought to meaning before speaking. In the example below, the student has a choice of what to say based on his or her general knowledge. The teacher writes the model on the board.

TEACHER: *(showing a picture of a horse and pointing to a student)* What about horses, Edwina?

STUDENT: Horses can jump but they can't fly.

Cats	can	run	and	can	walk
			but	can't	swim.

Expressing personal preferences

The examples above provide a certain amount of practice in the manipulation of the language and they do demand some attention to the meaning. However, such practice is, by its nature, remote from the way language is used for real purposes. After all the teacher knows very well that horses can jump but not fly! So why should the student say this? Simple practice of language points can often be achieved with a closer approximation to the use of language in order to communicate an idea. In the example below, the student is practising the use of 'would' but, at the same time, expressing his or her own preferences which the teacher could not have predicted. In this sense the student is telling the teacher something he or she did not know. A simple practice exercise is thus being used for real communicative purposes.

Two basic sentences could be written on the board:
I would prefer the orange.
I don't like either of them.

TEACHER: *(showing two pictures of fruit)* Which would you prefer, or perhaps you don't like either of them?
STUDENT: I would prefer the apple.
TEACHER: Fine

Note: Because the student is being asked to give a genuine response, it is only natural that you should respond to what he or she says in some way, even if it is only to smile and to say, 'fine', 'good', 'right', etc.

Mini role plays cued by pictures

In the above example the students are being asked to express their preferences. Pictures provide one way of stimulating and giving reference to such 'mini' but real conversations. An alternative is to have mini role plays in which the students pretend to be a character. What the students say is cued by the picture and might be in response to what is said to them. The teacher or another student might provide the other role.

TEACHER: What are you doing this evening, Roger? *(asking the question and then showing a picture of a basketball match)*
STUDENT: I'm going to a basketball match.
TEACHER: That's great!/How interesting!/Rather you than me! etc.

The slow picture reveal

The card can be put in an envelope and then withdrawn a centimetre at a time. As the students see more of the picture ask them to try to identify what they can see and to predict what might appear next in the picture. This gives guided practice in the use of descriptive language.

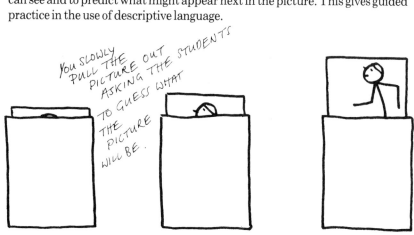

Open communicative practice

Characteristics and techniques: the cards can be juxtaposed rapidly.

Imagining connections

Show the students any two picture cards together and ask them to imagine a connection between them.

STUDENT: This man is driving home very quickly because he is hungry and wants his dinner.

Story connections

The example above can be extended into a story with each part of the story cued by the next picture (chosen at random). The pictures can be propped up on a shelf. Alternatively, they can be kept in the teacher's hand, in order. Each student who adds a sentence to the story must retell the story so far, cued by the pictures. Here is an example:

The man was driving home very quickly because he was hungry and wanted his dinner. He thought about his difficult job and he wished he could live on a desert island. He remembered his old friend Bill the Knife. He remembered that Bill loved ice cream. Suddenly he saw a dog in the road.

An alternative to the above example is to show the pictures to the students and to ask them to write for four minutes about each one. Insist that the writing links together as one story. At the end of the four minutes the students should take it in turns to read out their story to their neighbours. Ask one or two students to read out their story to the class as a whole.

Flashing a picture

Flash a picture card at the class at great speed and ask the students what they saw. Some will say they saw nothing, others will, amazingly, have seen something. Encourage differences of opinion and do not confirm or deny any ideas. Flash the picture again and ask the students to tell each other what they think they saw. Continue flashing, encouraging differences and debate. Finally show the picture.

Technical tips

1 The pictures must be clear enough to be seen the length of the classroom and at some speed. Magazine photographs may sometimes be too complicated and full of irrelevant detail. One way of reducing the distracting detail is to cut away the background leaving the main shape.

2 Line drawings should be simple and not sketchy. The lines should be quite thick, the shape should be as suggestive of the object as possible.

THIS SORT OF DIAGRAMMATIC DRAWING IS PERFECT FOR MOST LANGUAGE TEACHING NEEDS

A SKETCHY DRAWING IS DIFFICULT TO 'READ'

3 Colour should be used to make the shape stand out clearly and to contribute to recognition; for example, orange for an orange, yellow for a lemon. Sometimes colour can be used to draw attention to a small shape in the picture, for example, a small present; the rest of the picture can be drawn with black lines and the present can be brightly coloured. Just using colours for decorative purposes is probably a mistake in language teaching.

4 Card is expensive. Sometimes cheap 'offcuts' can be obtained free from a local printer. Otherwise use food packets or cut up cardboard boxes.

Word flash cards

Word flash cards are usually about 8 cm in height and are as long as is necessary for the text. They are principally, though not exclusively, used in the teaching of reading and writing.

Characteristics and techniques

1 Word flash cards are easy and inexpensive for the teacher to prepare.
2 The cards are easy to store and to carry to the classroom.
3 They are easy for the teacher and the students to handle and to use at the appropriate moment. They can be held, propped, or stuck to the board.
4 A number of cards can be displayed at the same time: by asking several students to hold them, by sticking them to the board, by clipping them to a wire (see technical tips page 118), by propping them on a shelf, by using a sentence maker. (See technical tips page 64.)

Presentation

Characteristics and techniques: the cards can be prepared by the teacher and/or students and may be handled and then stuck on different surfaces with adhesive plastic, sticky tape, pins, etc.

Labelling classroom objects

A well-established way of using word cards is for the teacher to stick them on objects in the classroom: the door, the cupboard, a window, a desk, etc. The intention is to familiarise the student with the written form of the word.

At the reading practice stage, a game could be played based on true/false in which the teacher moves the cards around before the students come into the classroom. The students must spot which words are in the wrong place and move them to the correct place.

Reading practice

Characteristics and techniques: strips of card or paper are easy and cheap to obtain and texts can readily be written on them with markers.

Dialogue sentence cards

Cards can be made of the sentences which have become familiar to the students in a short dialogue or in a story. These sentences can be shown as the dialogue is being spoken and then stuck on the board or held by students. This stage of recognition reading is modest in what it offers.

However, it is a well-tried technique and is particularly helpful to those students who are not only learning to read a foreign language but one with a different script.

Command cards

Another well-established use of word cards is 'commands'. Commands are written on the cards, the teacher shows a card to a student and the student carries out the command. The usual commands are: 'open the door', etc. However, more amusing commands could be added to the collection. For example:

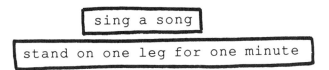

Writing practice

Characteristics and techniques: the ease and speed of selecting and displaying words and in any combination.

Class sentences

Word cards allow the teacher and class to build sentences and to experiment with the addition, the substitution and the subtraction of words within a sentence. The physical manipulation of the words can contribute enormously to an understanding of sentence construction by some students. (A variety of ways of learning should be offered to the class to match the variety of ways in which individual students need to learn.)

In the first example, successive students take a card, read it out to the class and then with the help of the class decide where they should stand in the sentence.

In the second example, the teacher asks the students to arrange the cards on the board to make a sentence. Here, one sentence is stuck on the board and another is propped on the shelf at the bottom of the board.

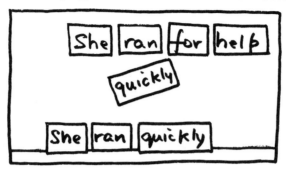

In the third example, the teacher gives a group of students a set of word cards and asks them to stand in alphabetical order.

Listening

Characteristics and techniques: the cards are easy and quick to make. They can be displayed at the most appropriate moment without technical difficulty.

Spot the word

The teacher reads or tells a story and the individual students hold up their cards as they hear their word spoken. This is training in intensive listening. The students are learning how to concentrate on one word or phrase and to ignore the rest.

The words might be selected by the teacher to reinforce a theme in the subject matter or in the language being used. For example, the students may have word cards representing the various ways in which narration can be connected: suddenly/then/next/ a few moments later/meanwhile/just at that moment/just before. Each student can be asked to note down how many times his or her word phrase is used. The frequency of use and the role of the words can then be discussed after the story.

Summarising a talk

Cards which summarise key points in a talk are most helpful in structuring the talk. They are useful in drawing attention to key points, in giving variety and interest in the talk, in acting as reminders of what the talk was about once it is over and in providing a reference for discussion.

The teacher (or students) might find this use of word cards helpful in reminding them of the order of points they have planned to make. And it also helps the listeners to understand the general argument of the talk and not to get lost.

The cards can be held up, pinned to soft board, stuck to the board with adhesive plastic, or propped along the blackboard shelf.

An example of a set of key points for a talk might be:

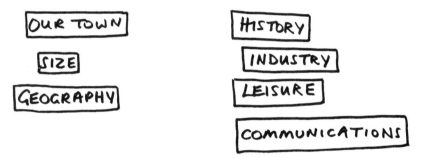

The same technique can also be used in story-telling. Each key creature or object can be named on a card:

Technical tips

1 Although card is stiffer and more durable than paper, paper strips are quite adequate.

2 Printers throw away enormous quantities of 'offcuts'. These are the strips of paper cut off the ends of printed sheets.

3 An alternative to producing individual cards is to have a number of standard length cards which are covered in a self-adhesive plastic. A water-based overhead projector pen can then be used to write words which can be wiped off later once the activity is over.

4 To establish a minimum height for the letters, try one out! That is the best way. However, the general guidance is that letters should be about 6 cm high to be seen 10 m away.

5 Words composed solely of CAPITAL LETTERS are more difficult to read than those in upper and lower case letters. We recognise words partly by their overall shape. Words made of capital letters all look the same shape, i.e. rectangular.

6 Ways of displaying word cards have been referred to above. A class display sentence maker can be made as follows:

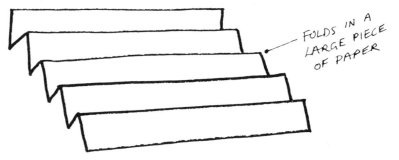

FOLDS IN A LARGE PIECE OF PAPER

A large sheet of paper is folded as shown above and then stapled onto card or hardboard.

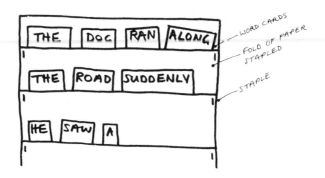

WORD CARDS
FOLD OF PAPER STAPLED
STAPLE

Workcards and worksheets

Workcards (about 15 cm × 20 cm) and worksheets are for individual student use or for use by students working in small groups. They provide an extremely useful base for the development of all four skills without the teacher's immediate involvement. Good course books provide a lot of this kind of material. However, many teachers make their own materials for students no matter how good their course book.

This type of visual material can be treated with a very wide range of techniques, only some of which can be exemplified here.

Note: For any individual and groupwork activities to be successful two things are necessary: 1 the students should understand what they have to do 2 the language demands on the students should be within their capabilities.

Standard exercise types

The following are all well-known types of exercise and are usually not too difficult and time-consuming for the teacher to prepare in the form of cards or sheets:

A text intended for translation
A text and comprehension questions
A text or a picture and multiple choice questions
A text or a picture and true/false statements
Sentences and/or pictures which must be matched
A picture to be described
Gapped texts to be completed
Jumbled texts (words or sentences to be arranged in the correct order)
Word games including crosswords, anagrams, etc.

Characteristics and techniques

2 Pictures, drawn by the teacher or by the students or taken from magazines, can be combined with texts either handwritten or typed or taken from authentic printed matter.
3 The two sides of the card can be used for presenting different information. This separation of the information is useful in certain types of activity.
4 A set of worksheets enables the teacher to set either individual or group tasks which students can perform more or less independently of the teacher.
5 The cards or sheets contribute to variety and interest in the classroom.

Controlled reading and writing practice

Characteristics and techniques: individual students can work at their own pace and level with their own workcard chosen by the teacher and/or themselves.

Handwriting and copy writing

Worksheets can be used to help students learn to write English script. Cards and sheets can be designed by the teacher to guide the student in the formation of individual letters and in the joining of letters. The students should, first of all, watch the teacher actually forming the letters on the board. (Some students have a natural ability to remember the sequence of movements you make, remembering in the way they might remember a sequence of dance steps.) The sheets or cards then offer individual guidance and memory support.

Note: If the student uses thin paper or places the master sheet on a window it is possible to trace over the letters.

Once the students have developed a reasonable degree of accuracy and control in letter formation and joining, encourage them to produce some personal writing, for example, writing their names or their friends' names.

Copy writing

The students should move on to more extended copying as well as more exploratory creative writing. Straightforward copying is mind numbing and not very useful! It is better to give a reason for copying. One reason for copying is to have a copy for oneself of a song or a poem. The student does not have to be familiar with all the language of the song but, of course, it would be sensible if he or she had heard it and liked it.

True/false copy writing

Copying does not need to be 'unthinking'! Various simple 'challenges' can require the student to think of the meaning of the text whilst actually only having to copy it. Simple challenges include: 1 only copy the true sentences 2 sort out the sentences into the correct order and then copy them 3 copy out the sentences which go together. These 'challenges' not only add interest and reason for using the language, but allow the teacher to use the technique for a higher proficiency level of student. In this example the student must only copy the true sentences.

I DON'T BELIEVE YOU

1 It was beautiful; there wasn't a cloud in the sky.
2 The path was easy to follow.
3 There was a bridge over the stream.
4 The stream was nearly empty.
5 John walked behind all the time.
6 I carried the haversack.

PICTURE: MAGAZINE PICTURE OR DRAWING

TRUE FALSE STATEMENTS HANDWRITTEN OR TYPED

Picture/text matching

Like many of the activities described above, this one can be done at a variety of levels. In this case the example has been chosen to demonstrate a picture/text matching activity suitable for an advanced level student.

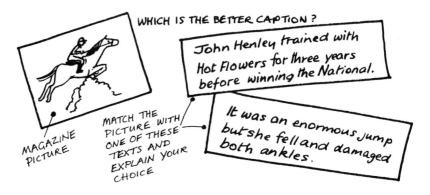

Text/text matching

Once more we have chosen to illustrate this type of activity with an example suitable for an advanced level student. Clearly, however, examples can be devised for any proficiency level.

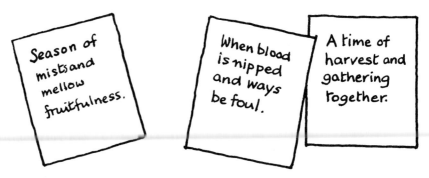

Gapped text

The gaps in the text can be chosen quite arbitrarily, but it is of more use to the student if you select gaps which focus on a skill (for example, the skill of guessing at the meaning of an unknown word from its position in the text) or on a language feature (for example, prepositions, pronouns, tense forms). The gap can be filled only by reading the text or might be filled by referring to a picture.

The text can, of course, be taken from the students' books, from authentic material or be written by you.

```
It --- unusually cold the day I ----
my wife.  The windows ------- as we
--- off but the visibility ---n't too
good.  When I --- that we ---- low on
petrol I ------- at a petrol station.
My wife ---- she would ----- the windows.
She ------- the front ones, lifting up
the wipers quite carefully.  Then she
---- round to the back of the car and
I never --- her again.  When she
---n't ---- back I ------- she must
---- ---- to the toilets.  But after
some time when she didn't ---- back I
--- out and ----- the attendant if he
had ---- her go into the toilets.  Then
I ----- a woman to go in to see if she
--- there.  She ---n't.  The attendant
didn't even seem to remember her getting
out of the car.
I ------ the police but they never ----
her.
```

Jumbled texts

The texts might be single word cards. These could be kept together in an envelope and used for sentence building. You might challenge the student to build the longest sentence possible with the words in the envelope or to build as many sentences as possible in five mintues, copying down each one before starting to build another.

Controlled and guided oral practice

Characteristics and techniques: workcards and worksheets can provide motivation, guidance and reference for groupwork.

There are various established techniques for organising controlled oral practice in groups. These include:

Pictures cues for use in mini dialogues
Texts and/or pictures guiding role play
Information-gap activities
Pictures and/or texts to be matched, grouped or ordered
Game-like activities
Questionnaires

Picture cued mini dialogues

Pictures can be cues in mini dialogues (two to six exchanges). This type of activity has enormous potential for the teacher.

However, for it to be efficient the teacher must build up a collection of magazine pictures and keep them filed by subject.

Pictures can be used to cue answers to questions or to provide cues for substitutions in sentences. First of all ensure that the students know what they are supposed to do and check that they have the language to do it. This can be done by doing sample mini dialogues in front of the class.

In most cases there should be four to six students in the group around a table.

A pile of pictures is placed face down on the table and the students study a mini dialogue and the instructions about what they have to do. They then take part in the dialogue, picking up the pictures as directed and using them to determine what they might say.

The dialogues can be at a variety of levels. Here are two. The first is highly-controlled practice at beginners' level. The second is more demanding as the follow up is not guided but it is left to the student to express any idea he or she feels is appropriate.

The students are guided by a mini dialogue card:

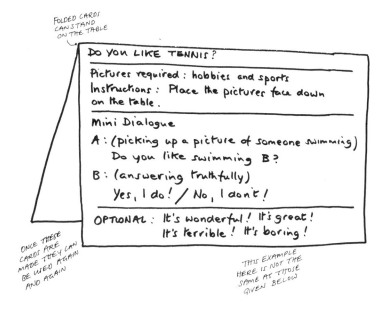

FOLDED CARDS CAN STAND ON THE TABLE

DO YOU LIKE TENNIS?

Pictures required : hobbies and sports
Instructions : Place the pictures face down on the table.

Mini Dialogue

A : (picking up a picture of someone swimming)
   Do you like swimming B?

B : (answering truthfully)
   Yes, I do! / No, I don't!

OPTIONAL : It's wonderful! It's great!
   It's terrible! It's boring!

ONCE THESE CARDS ARE MADE THEY CAN BE USED AGAIN AND AGAIN

THIS EXAMPLE HERE IS NOT THE SAME AS THOSE GIVEN BELOW

Elementary level
A pile of pictures of hobbies and sports

STUDENT A: *(picking up a picture of someone playing tennis)* Do you like tennis?

STUDENT B: *(answering truthfully and choosing from the range of responses given)* Yes, very much./I quite like it./I don't like it very much./I hate it!

The dialogue continues by students picking up a card and then asking another student a similar question.

INSTRUCTION CARD

PICTURES UPSIDE DOWN

Intermediate level

A pile of pictures from other countries

STUDENT A: *(picking up a picture of Rome)* Would you like to go to Rome?
STUDENT B: *(answering truthfully)* Yes, I would.
STUDENT A: Why?
STUDENT B: Because I would like to visit the ancient buildings and I would like to see Michelangelo's ceiling in the Sistine Chapel.

Dialogue, role play and simulation

Dialogue and role play are well-established activities in language teaching. They are relatively easy to prepare by the teacher and students and provide intensive and useful language practice. Changes to the dialogues can be cued by text and/or pictures.

If your class are not familiar with dialogue and role play it is advisable to begin by writing the model dialogue on the chalkboard. All the examples given below could be written on the chalkboard; indeed, as we have seen (pages 14 and 15) the chalkboard offers the teacher great flexibility in adapting the examples below from one type to another.

Many designs of role play card have been developed in recent years. A few basic types are illustrated in the examples below, roughly graded according to the difficulties they present to the student. Each gives a different level of control over what is said.

Note: You should give as much attention as possible to the design of the cards or sheets. Any difficulty in using them can demoralise the students and reduce the usefulness of the activity. In the examples below some basic design decisions have been made to:

- give character and interest to the dialogues by the addition of faces;
- separate the texts from each other and to keep their order clear by the following means:
    1. using different styles of writing
    2. using enclosing speech balloons
    3. using two thicknesses of line
    4. overlapping the speech balloons
    5. using direction flow lines
    6. using tones.

Repetition dialogue

In this type of role play the students read out the dialogue as it is given.

Substitution dialogues

In this type the students choose what to say from what is given.

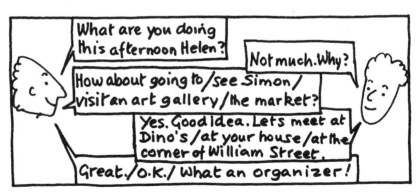

Symbol dialogue

Some of the words are replaced by abbreviating and/or by symbols and/or
blanks. It is important to ensure that the class understand the conventions
used. It is essential to explain or even to work out the symbols with the class
before they are used.

Key word cue dialogue

What the students say is represented by a single key word or symbol.

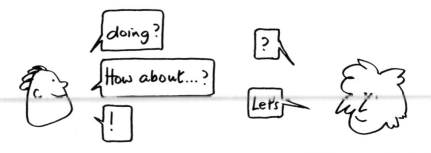

Flowchart instruction dialogue

The students are directed what to say by an instruction. This is probably the
most difficult type of cue. The student must be able to read and understand a
rather abbreviated and abstract direction and produce an appropriate
utterance using different language and in a natural way.

The particular design of flowchart made use of here is one of the most useful designs as it is clear how the dialogue progresses. The paper can be folded down the middle so that each student can only see his or her own part.

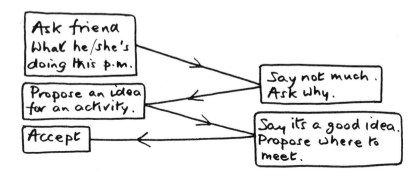

Branching flowchart dialogue

This technique allows the student to choose, to some degree, what direction the dialogue should take.

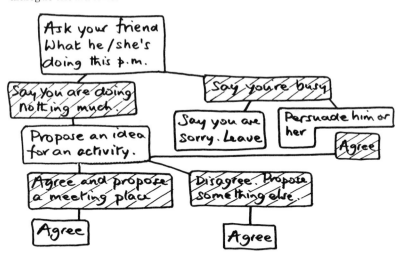

Simulation

In a simulation, each student takes on the role of a fictional character in an imaginary situation. Dialogues are not specified and they cannot be predicted. Simulations can be evolved by the teacher together with the students quite easily. The most basic simulation only requires a situation and a number of characters to be described.

If there are six characters then there must be six students in the group to play out the simulation, i.e. six worksheets are required plus one which all the students can see describing the situation. The students read and study the description on their cards or sheets and then take part in the discussion which follows as if they were the person on the card.

Situation

A group of six people are visiting a tourist town. They have arrived in the evening and are asked to make decisions about what they would like to do the next day.

Edwina Rice

Seventy-five years old. Likes visiting art galleries and museums. Can't walk very far.

Dennis Hall

In his forties. Likes sport, particularly golf and tennis. No interest in museums. Enjoys eating out.

Maggie Steel

Nineteen years old. Enjoys walking and swimming. Also interested in art and music.

Information-gap activities

This type of activity is now closely identified with the emphasis placed on using language for the purposes of communication in the classroom. In fact, although information-gap activities include some useful devices, they are effectively games rather than the sort of things people do in their normal daily dealings with each other. Four examples based on the difference between two sets of information which are easy for the teacher to devise are summarised here. Other examples of information-gap activities can be found elsewhere. (See other volumes in the Keys series.)

What's the difference?

In this version of an information-gap activity there should be two lots of information stuck on either side of a piece of card. (Alternatively, the information can be on two different cards.) The information should be similar but not identical. Students working in pairs sit either side of the card (one of them holding it so that they can each see one side). There are many possible variations of this idea.

In this example, the students have two similar pictures. They could be two magazine photographs of similar scenes or similar lots of people. The students' job is to jot down as many differences as they can find between the two sets of information in five mintues. The student not holding the picture must do the writing!

Matching activities

There are a large number of versions of this useful and productive type of activity. Here are a few of them:

Pelmanism

A group of students work together sitting around a table. They are given an even number of cards (twenty is sufficient). The cards are paired; for example, there may be a picture of fruit on one card and on the other card will be its name. The students study all the cards, mix them together and then turn them face down on the table in neat rows. The students are allowed to see where each picture (or word card) is being laid. The students then take it in turns to point to the back of two cards claiming them to be a pair. If the student is right, then he or she keeps them. For example:

STUDENT A: This is a picture of a pineapple *(turning it over . . . and it is!)* and this is the word, 'pineapple' *(turning it over . . . and it is!)* Yes!

If the student is not right, both cards are left in the same place and turned back again.

Search for your twin

In this matching activity, each student in the class is given a piece of paper with a text and/or a picture on it. He or she must search for another student in the class with the matching paper. The same kind of pairs can be used as in Pelmanism; other types of pairs include:

Questions/answers

How are you?   Not very well.

Words/dictionary definitions

Cat | a small domesticated mammal kept as a pet to catch rats or mice

Poets/extracts from their poems

Hardy | O the opal and the sapphire

First half of a sentence/second half of a sentence

He was cold because he had | been waiting for more than 3 hours.

Picture of actions/sentences describing actions

 She's shopping

Present tense form of a verb/past tense form of the same verb

do | did

American English word/British English word

elevator | lift

Questionnaires

Questionnaires provide a rich source of activities which focus on particular language features, most obviously the question form, and are also seen as activities which are interesting in themselves.

The questionnaire illustrated here contains some questions that make use of elementary vocabulary and structure and yet could lead to an interesting statistical survey. Other questions are more personal and would lead to further discussion.

What time do you go to bed?
How much sleep do you really need?
Do you like sleeping?
Do you ever sleep during the day?
Do you snore?
Do you dream?
Can you remember your dreams?
Do you have some dreams again and again?
What is your favourite dream?
Do you have nightmares?
What was your worst nightmare?
What is the longest time you have slept?
What is the longest time you have been awake?
Do you sleep with the window open?
Are you bright and fresh when you wake up?
Do you exercise when you get up?

Free oral practice

Characteristics and techniques: there are a number of standard techniques on worksheets and workcards which can be used in groupwork for promoting conversation, discussion, extended description and story-telling. These techniques include:

Speculating about a picture
Discussing a topic with reference to pictures and/or texts
Expressing feelings and talking about personal experiences based on a picture
  or a text
Story-telling based on a series of pictures and/or texts

Speculating

The students first of all describe what they see in the picture and then
speculate about what might be happening. In practice the two stages overlap
because people do not all 'read' a picture in the same way. In this sense what is
description for one person might be speculation for another.

The workcard should have a picture and two sets of questions. To involve oral
work, two students can be asked to work together. Even more oral work is
involved if the following organisation is adopted. Have two pairs of students (A
and B; C and D). Each pair should work on one workcard. After an agreed
amount of time the pairs exchange cards and work on their 'new' card in the
same way. After another agreed amount of time make new pairs of A and C
and B and D. Each student explains to the other student what ideas they had
about each of the cards.

1 How old is this person?

2 What is he doing now?

3 What is his job?

4 What sort of personality does he have?

5 What other things can you imagine about him?

MAGAZINE PICTURE SHOWING A PERSON IN AN INFORMATIVE SETTING

QUESTIONS PROMPTING SPECULATION AND DISCUSSION

An alternative to using a picture of a person is to use a picture of a place, perhaps a picture postcard of a town. The students work in pairs to try to analyse the picture and to deduce as much as they can about the place: industries/size of town/which country/north or south/climate/ etc.

In this case the answer need not be speculative. If you have the facts about the place, these could be written on another card. Which pair of students was able to deduce the more accurately?

Free writing

Characteristics and techniques: it is relatively easy for the teacher to find pictures which can be cut from magazines, etc. and to find or to write texts which can be pasted onto cards for stimulating writing: description and analysis, speculation, expression, story-telling.

Some types of material include:

Artistic, stimulating pictures which stir the imagination;
Ambiguous pictures which can be interpreted in a variety of ways;
A series of pictures or diagrams which describe a process;
Sample letters and suggestions for equivalent letters;
Texts with gaps which can be filled in creatively, with single words, phrases, dialogues or whole paragraphs. In this type of activity there is no one correct answer.

Technical tips

1 If you have smooth card you can write directly on it. If you are using card cut from packets, etc. then you should paste onto it typed, photocopied or handwritten texts. If you make a lot of workcards or worksheets then it is helpful to give each one a code which you write in the same place on the sheet. It is also helpful if all the cards and sheets are made to standard sizes which fit into file boxes, spring files, etc.

2 Card is clearly more attractive and durable if it is covered in transparent clear adhesive plastic or kept in a clear plastic bag.
If you can reproduce sheets easily you may feel they are easier to produce than cards and can be replaced more easily. Cards can be lost, taken by students and not returned, etc. and then your hard work is lost!

3 Students can sometimes be asked to conceive, design, write and illustrate cards and sheets which are then used either within the same class or in lower classes. If the students know that their work will be used, they are more likely to do their best and they will see the sense in your insisting that the final version is correct. The act of making teaching material is one of the best ways of learning! It is thus not a waste of the students' time to ask them to do this. They might like to sign the workcards or worksheets with their names.

4 If you can share the work of producing worksheets with other teachers it would clearly be a big help.

5 You are not supposed to make multiple copies of published materials. However, you can cut up two Students' Books and mount each exercise on a piece of card. If the card is then laminated you will have a most valuable and flexible resource pack which will help you to deal with a variety of needs in your class at the same time and for little cost.

6 Instructions on the card or sheet must be as clear as possible or the students will waste time and disruption will be caused. If necessary give the instructions in the mother tongue. The main thing is that the activity should be well done.

7 Be sure that you know roughly how long the work should take. If the work is over in a minute it is probably not worth doing because of the disproportionate amount of time spent organising it. On the other hand more than fifteen minutes may be too long without some sort of interaction with you.

8 If the cards or sheets are for the students to keep, they can be encouraged to illustrate them, colour them or add graphic symbols to them.

9 For suggestions on layout and lettering see pages 100 to 108.

Authentic printed materials

Authentic printed materials include anything written and printed in English: newspapers, magazines, publicity, technical instructions for equipment, holiday brochures, etc.

Characteristics and techniques

1 Very often, free material is available to the teacher.
2 The fact that it is authentic material clearly not produced for schools means that students are often motivated by it and curious.
3 The complexity of the language is a disadvantage only if you expect the students to understand every word. It is not the difficulty of the text which determines which proficiency level of students can use the text, but the task you give them to do. For example, you could give a newspaper article to a first year group of students and ask them to find how many words they can recognise. Thus one should be exploiting the complexity of the material and showing students that they can often make some sense even of difficult material if they look for every possible clue. The material should not be used for testing comprehension but for teaching comprehension which means developing a positive and confident attitude to it and learning some basic techniques for dealing with a lot of language which is difficult to understand.
4 The material can usually be photocopied and then stuck onto card for reuse.
5 The material is often much more expensively produced than educational books available to teachers in many countries.

Newspapers

Characteristics and techniques: the very fact that the language of newspapers is difficult to read is one of the reasons for using them. Students must experience the flow of native language use and know how to do their best with it.

The topicality of newspapers is relevant and so too is the reflection of the culture.

Here are a few things you can do with most newspapers.

With your beginners:
1 Ask them to list all the words they recognise.

DOZENS of pensioners have been left out in the cold as plans to move into luxury retirement flats have fallen through at the last minute.

Wimpey Homes Holdings Ltd., opened their recently-completed Parkfield Court development in Didsbury two months ago for a public viewing.

2 Ask them to guess what each article is about either broadly, for example, sport or more specifically, for example, the London marathon.

3 Ask them to identify the different sections of the newspaper: the main news, the editorial, general features, sport, business, advertisements, etc.

With more advanced students:

1 Prepare some questions based on different parts of the newspaper which do not entail the students reading everything in detail but only in searching for the answers to your questions. (Advanced students could be asked to prepare the questions for less advanced students.) For example:

- How much does the 1987 Ford Granada cost and how many miles has it done?

B **ASTRA GTE 1.8i**, all white, white alloy wheels, full history £4795
(C) **SUZUKI SJ413 JEEP.** 1300cc. Gunmetal grey metallic. Hard & Soft tops. Superb 4-wheel driving for only £4995

EXECUTIVE
87 **FORD GRANADA GL**, new model, Gold Metallic, ABS brakes, 20,000 miles £6995
86 **VAUXHALL CARLTON.** Gold metallic, one owner, low mileage, pristine example £4995
89 **RENAULT 25 GTS AUTOMATIC**, Lagoon Blue, Save £1,500 on new £11750
85 **RENAULT 25 GTX**, Lagoon Blue, alarm, sunroof, full service history................................. £5995

- What time is *Gone With the Wind* on the television?
- Who lost their cat?
- What did Sarah Raphael say when her painting was sold to the Metropolitan Museum of Modern Art in New York?

2 Give the students advertisements from a newspaper showing prices of, for example, houses, cars, TVs, etc. and advertisements for jobs showing salaries. Ask questions such as:

- How much do things cost in Britain (or the country of origin of the newspaper)?
- How do these prices relate to what people earn, judging by the advertisements for jobs?
- How do these prices and incomes relate to those in your own country?

DIRECTOR
AROUND £30,000
+ GOOD CAR
WITNEY, OXON

MEDICAL SECRETARY

This challenging and interesting post involves responsibility for the provision of a secretarial service to a Professor of Gynaecology and his team.

Shorthand and typing skills are essential as is previous medical secretarial experience.

Hours of work: 37 per week, Monday to Friday.

Salary: £5,484 rising by annual increments to £6,474, plus proficiency allowances of shorthand and typing up to a maximum of £573 where appropriate.

Informal enquiries welcome for both positions. Please contact Christine Tomlins on 061-276 6999. Closing date: 28 April 1989.

86 **VOLVO 340 GL**, 5-door, Navy Blue, 20,000 miles, very clean example............................. £4995
(D) **ROVER 216 SE**, Black, 17,000 miles, top of the range, every extra, superb example................ £5795
86 **FIESTA POPULAR PLUS 1.1** In maroon, 14,000 miles, fantastic condition.................... £3795
(E) **FIAT UNO 1.3SX**, Black, central locking, electric windows................................ £5495
(C) **FIAT UNO 55 SUPER**, in white, full service history. A lovely little car.......................... £3495
85 **FORD FIESTA 1.1 DASH**, in black, special edition model, excellent condition........................ £3495

3 Cut out several headlines and ask the students to discuss what the article might be about. This is a good way of developing predictive reading skills.

4 Cut out several headlines and articles and ask the students to match them.

5 Cut out several photographs and their captions separately. Ask the students to match them. One approach to this technique is to give a photograph to a pair of students and to ask them to note down as much as they can surmise from a study of the picture. They should then write a short article or caption to go with it before being shown the actual one used.

6 Cut up an article into several pieces and ask the students to sequence the pieces correctly. This can be done in various ways. In one version the class is divided into small groups and each is given one section of an article. They study it and try to make sense of it. Then the teacher asks each group to read out their piece of the article. The groups make notes on the other pieces they hear and try to decide what order they should be in. Next there is a class discussion. The pieces can be read and re-read until everyone is in agreement. Finally the whole article is read out.

Festival under way

Plans for a tenth anniversary celebration of Didsbury Festival are well under way. It will be held on Saturday May 13 at 2.00pm.

"There will be something there for everyone to enjoy". The day will start with a procession and floats travelling along school Lane, through the village and into Didsbury park.

The committee are still looking for people who wish to take part in the procession or hire a stall.

They also want to encourage local shopkeepers and businesses to decorate their shop windows along the route to support the event.

A number of side stalls, children's fun fair and a 1920s

For further information contact Phil Gunn on 445 0793.

Festival committee chair Eileen Cropper said: "Its been a lot of hard work but we hope this will be the best festival yet.

jazz band will feature. And a pet show, Morris Dancers Popmobility and a Punch and Judy show will also be included.

7 The students study an article or a letter to the editor and try to rewrite it in a way which expresses a different point of view.

Sir,

In recent years there has been more and more criticism of dogs and dog owners. Some of this criticism may be reasonable. However, there is no reason why dog owners should be ashamed of having a dog. Dogs, like all pets, provide a social service: lonely people have a companion to care for; people who would otherwise become unfit, have to take their dogs for a walk.

A free country means a free country for people and their pets to live out their lives as they want to, providing, of course, that they do not interfere with the lives of other people.

Anthony Higgins
12 Belfield Road
Manchester M20 0BH

---

8 Study two articles on the same topic and discuss the different views expressed.
9 Photocopy an article and use typists' correction fluid to remove items from it. You could remove: punctuation, language items such as articles, conjunctions or prepositions. Photocopy the article with the gaps and give it to the students, asking them to work out what is missing. Finally let them compare their effort with the original.

HELP THE AGED

Volunteers urgently needed to help with jobs at the Help the Aged shop on Paletine Road, Northenden. They needed to help with sort goods, iron clothes, serv customers and other tasks.

The shop manager would be delighted to hear from anyone who can spare at least a morning or an afternoon a week. The shop staffed almost entirely by volunteers and cannot operate without such support.

10 Ask the students to examine the way that journalists use English. This can be done in pairs and then in groups before the class pool all their observations, for example, infinitives used to express future, use of alliteration, passives, etc. They could then make a list of useful expressions and of clichés which you would prefer not to use.

Publicity material

Publicity material includes: the advertisements of major industries, the small 'ads' (advertising rooms to rent, jobs, work, etc.), propaganda (health care and road safety).

The language is often succinct; on the other hand, it is often so colloquial as to be obscure except to the likely customers of the product.

Characteristics and techniques: there are two main aspects to the use of publicity material, firstly a study of the nature of persuasion, of the assumption of values, of stereotyping, etc. and secondly the language, both pictorial and verbal, which is used.

Here are a few things you can do with most beginners:
1 Show the students a number of advertisements and ask them what idea, experience or object is being advertised and who the publicity is aimed at. How is the advertiser trying to persuade people? Beginners can be allowed to use their mother tongue for this analysis. The learning derives from their analysis of the advertisement and from their preparation to do this kind of analysis in the foreign language at a later date.
2 Ask the students to list all the words and phrases in the material that they know.

3 Ask the students to note down how often certain key words are used.
4 Give the students (orally or written on the board) a number of slogans and ask them to say what product they are referring to.

For more advanced students:

1 Ask the students to think of what should be promoted in their country (health, safety, leisure, etc.) and produce some ideas for it. The ideas might include text and pictures for posters, slogans, badges, direct mail leaflets, news broadcasts (done as two-minute cassette tape recordings).
2 Ask the students to study an advertisement for a product or experience (holidays, restaurant, sports centre) and write a letter of complaint to the manager about the object they have bought or about their imagined experience there.

Dear Sir,

I went on your tour of the South Coast. It was terrible! The bus driver was drunk and crazy. He watched the television while he was driving! And the hotels! The beds were full of insects. I want my money back.

Yours faithfully,
Anthony Higgins

3 Ask the students to analyse the language: the way it is used, the use of metaphor, colloquialisms; the use of imperatives or more persuasive language, advice, suggestions; the use of the word 'you' impersonal and personal. What 'tone of voice' is used?
4 Ask the students to produce an alternative advertisement which would be more appropriate for a particular social group they know.
5 Ask the students to write, for amusement's sake, an advertisement which would sell as little of the product as possible.

THE SMALLEST CHOICE!
THE WORST SERVICE!
1% CUSTOMER SATISFACTION
GUARANTEED!

6 Ask the students to write an advertisement pretending that one of the other students in the class is a product. They can use the language of advertising which they have noted in earlier tasks.

Judith is A1 quality! She has few miles on the clock. She starts quickly on cold mornings. She is comfortable but she has a high top speed.

You would be proud of her if she was parked outside your house.

7 Give the students copies of holiday brochures. Ask them to choose a holiday to go on with their friend. They should say what each of them will enjoy, how much it will cost and when they have chosen to go. They could be asked to choose a holiday for someone else in the same way.

Technical tips

1 Sources of material
   In your country English language newspapers may be available either from an English-speaking country or produced locally.
   Much publicity material and many equipment instructions are in English.
   You might be able to get material in English from firms in your country owned by companies from English-speaking countries.
   You might be able to get materials from the embassies of English-speaking countries.
   In many countries the British Council/USIS and the equivalent institutions from other English-speaking countries have arrangements with teachers to use their libraries.
   If you have friends in an English-speaking country they can send you printed material through the post at a cheap rate.
2 Organisation in the classroom
   You are unlikely to get enough copies of newspapers or publicity leaflets, etc. for every student. There are several ways of dealing with this limitation:
   (a) You can give a newspaper to a pair or group to work on while other groups work on different tasks altogether.
   (b) You can cut the newspaper up and give out parts of it to different pairs or groups.

(c) You can cut out certain articles or parts of articles and paste those on a sheet of paper and make a photocopy of that (for purposes of research).

(d) You can separate the pages and display these on the classroom walls or on tables. Students must then study the paper where it is displayed and with this arrangement a lot of students can work from one single copy of a newspaper or from several examples of publicity material displayed in the same way.

The learning environment

By far the richest material available to the language teacher lies in the learning environment. Only a few of the possibilities sketched out below can be illustrated in this book.

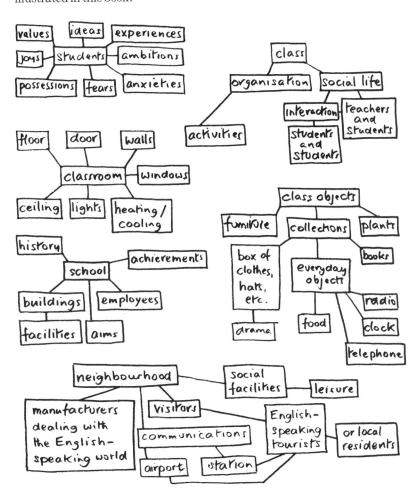

Characteristics and techniques

Because this is such a varied and rich source of material only a few pointers can be given here.

1 The learning environment is a living society which the students care about in one way or another. They are also knowledgeable about their environment in many respects. They know some things you do not know, for example, about themselves, about their families and friends and very probably about parts of the neighbourhood, about jobs, leisure and so on. For these reasons there is much to exploit in the learning environment. The question for some teachers and students might be: Why do this in the foreign language? It is a fair question if asked! One answer would be, because it is interesting and lets us see if we can talk about such things in the foreign language, i.e. it is a personal challenge. Another response might be: Let's prepare ourselves for dealing with foreign visitors to our neighbourhood who we could help.

2 For the most part the resources of the learning environment are readily available, varied and free!

Life in the classroom

Characteristics and techniques

1 Language course books try to represent real people in real life situations. The classroom is one part of the real, and very visual, world. In every class there is a wealth of experience, of opinions and of ideas. It is rarely tapped in traditional teaching.

Normally a teacher's knowledge and experience is much greater than a young student's. Nevertheless, each student has his or her own experiences, hopes, ambitions, anxieties, joys and possessions which are evidenced in visual information such as personal appearance, personal possessions, abilities, and by reference to visual experience outside the classroom. The fact that these are different to those of other students in the class (to a greater or lesser extent) means that there are 'information gaps', 'opinion gaps', 'experience gaps', and various other 'gaps' which provide the very reason we need for speaking and listening, reading and writing.

2 In every culture there is a different level of willingness to share personal information. Only you can be the judge of how much the students might be willing to share. Nevertheless, it is usually the case that students are willing to share more than is traditionally expected of them providing what they say is treated with respect and is given value.

3 The relationship between the students and between you and the students is different in most cultures. This is an opportunity for you to contextualise

levels of formality and informality of language in a way that the students can understand, for example, greetings: Good morning; . . . . Hi!

4 The organisation of the class and the lesson provides considerable opportunity for the teacher to contextualise language.

Here are some ways of talking about the visual aspects of life in the classroom.

Oh,	I like	your Pam's	dress. shirt. new hairstyle.	It's very nice!

Hannah,	you	don't	look very pleased.	What is it? What's wrong?

Whose is this	book? bag?	I found it	on on	my desk. the floor.

Barbara, Gordon,	would you	clean the board for me put these books in the cupboard	please?

Please	move your desks together. put your chairs in a circle.

Tell me about	your picture. your favourite film. the most horrible thing you have ever seen.

(showing a picture)

What do you think they are	doing? saying? thinking?

The classroom, its furniture and objects

Characteristics and techniques: there is a floor, a ceiling, a door and there are walls and windows in most classrooms. There are usually desks, chairs, chalkboards, cupboards. There are the possessions of the students. Sometimes there are plants. And there could be a collection of food packets, some fruit, a bicycle, and basic equipment for simple scientific experiements. For drama there can be a collection of old clothes, scarves, hats and an old telephone. These objects can be used in various ways:

1 They can be used for what they are: students can be asked to name objects and describe their qualities, to open and close windows and so on.

2 The origin and manufacture of the objects can be analysed.

3 The objects can be used as symbols and metaphors: an ancient method of teaching. One brick on its own is of limited use, together they make a wall. Words related together offer meaning, whereas on their own they are fairly useless. Bricks must be joined just as thoughts must be linked, etc.
The teacher might suggest that the front wall of the classroom represents the present time, the two side walls represent past time touching present time and the back wall is an identifiable period of time in the past.

4 The objects in the room can be subjected to the fantasy and imagination of the students. For example, the ideas below came from a class of fourteen year olds when the teacher showed them an ordinary exercise book and said, This is not an exercise book, what is it? The students, sometimes combining the exercise book with mime claimed the following:

STUDENT A: *(putting it on his head)* It's a hat.

STUDENT B: *(holding the bottom and swinging it)* It's a tennis racquet.
STUDENT C: *(holding it in front of her eyes)* It's a television.
STUDENT D: *(holding it on one long edge as if it were heavy)* It's a suitcase.
STUDENT E: *(holding it up on all five fingers of one hand)* It's an umbrella.
STUDENT F: *(rolling it and peeling it)* It's a banana.
STUDENT G: *(rolling it and writing with it)* It's a pen.
STUDENT H: *(rolling it and looking through it)* It's a telescope.
STUDENT I: *(rolling it with one end small and placing it in a vase)* It's a bunch of flowers.
STUDENT J: *(opening it out)* It's an aeroplane.
STUDENT K: *(opening it out and flapping the pages)* It's a bird.
STUDENT L: *(opening it out and blowing his nose on it)* It's a handkerchief.

Here are a few more ideas for each of the above types of object:

Walls

Obviously walls invite displays of wallpictures and posters of student collages and writings and of charts explaining points of grammar. All of these make a creative language environment. This is difficult if you do not have your own classroom.

Student possessions

These can be identified, named and analysed with regard to performance, origin, cost, sentimental value, associated experiences, etc.

Plants

A seed can be planted and language used to organise its survival and to record its progress.

Everyday objects

Everyday objects can be identified and evaluated, and their cost, availability, efficiency, and students' personal preferences can be discussed. Their qualities can be compared. They can be used in role play.

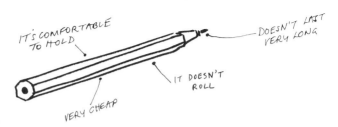

Interesting objects

We become familiar with everyday objects and don't think about their potential in language teaching. For example, we can get students involved in tuning a radio to see how many stations are broadcasting in English, or trying to identify different languages and what the people might be talking about.

Old clothes

Old hats, scarves and coats together with old telephones and other everyday objects can be used in drama, either in controlled role play or in creative drama. For example, give out a range of hats, perhaps a trilby, a flat hat, a beret, a rainhat, a crash helmet, a baby's hat, a flowery, old-fashioned lady's hat. Ask the students to work out characters, a situation and a dialogue to play for the others.

Furniture

Chairs arranged around a table at the front of the class become a café. Chairs in a line represent a bus.

The school

Characteristics and techniques: the class is usually part of a school which itself is a complex community. The organisation and social life of the school, the people and their roles, and the school buildings and facilities are important in the life of the student. Experiences, knowledge and opinions about the school can be the subject of conversation and discussion in the class. Here are a few examples of what can be done.

Drawing plans

Drawing plans of the school and naming the parts. This is not an easy task, particularly if the students are unused to making plans. It is rich in its language potential.

The work of people in the school

Director, office staff, caretaking staff, technicians and teachers. What do they have to do? A natural context for the present habitual! Also 'what happens if' you break your arm, etc. Produce a booklet about the school for foreign visitors. Cover its history, location, facilities, aims, achievements, plans, etc.

The school neighbourhood

Characteristics and techniques: most of the students will be from the neighbourhood of the school or will be familiar with it. Once more, it is a potentially rich resource for the teacher. Here are some suggestions:

- How well do the students know their neighbourhood? Ask them to try to remember and to describe everything they can see from the front gate of the school or what they can see if they stand on the town hall steps.
- Help them to prepare a study of the neighbourhood in English: employment, leisure, history, geography, climate, etc. This might be done for the town hall to give away to visitors.
- Ask them to work out a guide for tourists, giving a plan, location of facilities, times, costs, etc.
- Ask the students to collect any examples of the use of English in the neighbourhood.
- If there are any English-speaking visitors to the neighbourhood invite them to the school. Prepare the class by getting each student to make up a question to put to the visitor.
- If there are any firms or institutions in the area which deal with English-speaking countries, see what experience they have and if you could use it in your lessons.
- If there is an airport, consider taking your students there and studying where the planes are travelling to, and interviewing passengers and airport staff if that is possible. It is advisable to arrange the visit to the airport before you go!

10 Production tips

Designing

Teachers design every time they write or draw on the chalkboard or produce a worksheet. The question is not whether you design but whether you do it well or badly. Visual design is an aspect of communication. It is no more justifiable to say that visual design is unimportant than it is to say that speaking or writing are unimportant.

Artistic and communicative talent?

Yes, artistic and communicative talent are necessary and, thank goodness, we all have this talent! (I admit that some have it more strongly than others.)

A lot can be achieved by simply making use of our common sense or common talent.

Two things to concentrate on:

1 Clarity of information. The student should be able to see what you want him or her to see.
2 Expression. The style in which the information is presented affects how we respond to the meaning. There is a dignified way of speaking, of moving and of designing a page. There are ways of speaking, moving and designing pages which can express a wide variety of feelings: excitement, humour, modernity, conflict, gloom, mystery, caring and consideration.

The suggestions on the following pages apply to the design of all the visual materials referred to in this book.

Layout

Layout of your information (text and/or pictures) on the chalkboard, on worksheets, on wallpictures and in exhibitions and displays, etc.

Designers usually base their layouts on grids. Grids give a sense of organisation to the information. The vertical and horizontal 'lining up' of information is the basis of the grid. If this is done very strictly, the effect is formal. If photographs or titles span more than one column of the grid then a certain informality is introduced. More informality is introduced if the pictures are not rectangular but cutout shapes or if the text is placed at an angle. Many teachers would like to project an image of themselves which is friendly but nevertheless authoritative and organised. The right choice of grid and way of using it can reflect this. Here are some basic grids which you can use:

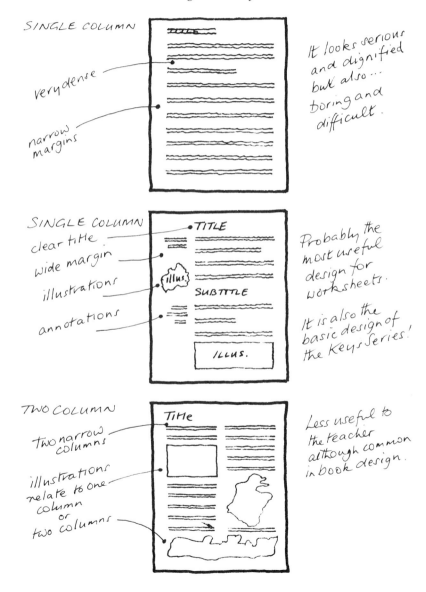

SINGLE COLUMN

very dense

narrow margins

It looks serious and dignified but also... boring and difficult.

SINGLE COLUMN

clear title.

wide margin

illustrations

annotations

Probably the most useful design for worksheets.

It is also the basic design of the Keys series!

TWO COLUMN

Two narrow columns

illustrations relate to one column or two columns

Less useful to the teacher although common in book design.

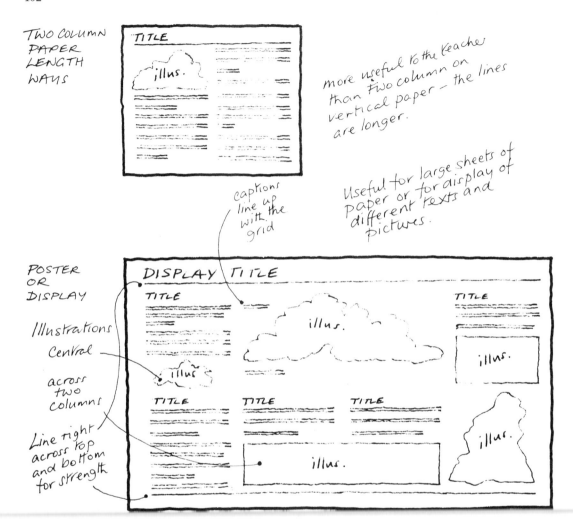

TWO COLUMN
PAPER
LENGTH
WAYS

TITLE

illus.

more useful to the teacher
than two column on
vertical paper – the lines
are longer.

captions
line up
with the
grid

Useful for large sheets of
paper or for display of
different texts and
pictures.

POSTER
OR
DISPLAY

Illustrations
Central

across
two
columns

Line right
across top
and bottom
for strength

DISPLAY TITLE

TITLE

illus.

illus

TITLE

illus.

TITLE

TITLE

TITLE

illus.

illus.

The suggestions on the following pages apply to the design of workcards, wallpictures, OHP transparencies and displays and exhibitions.

Pictures

Pictures need not always be placed strictly within the grid. They might be allowed to go off the paper altogether. The edge of the paper then contributes to the verticality or horizontality of the design and gives great strength but with a feeling of variety and informality.

Pictures need not always be rectangular. The character of an object is often better shown by cutting out its shape and this contributes to the overall richness of effect.

 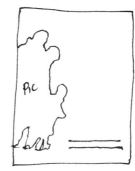 

Grouping and reading direction

Grouping

The following features help to group information; they are not all necessary:

- a separate heading;
- space at the top and bottom;
- a line at top and bottom or an enclosing line box;
- a line drawn vertically to separate it from nearby information;
- a different typeface or style of lettering;
- a different background tone or colour;
- the proximity of a caption to its illustration.

Reading direction

Most people familiar with roman script want to read from left to right and from top to bottom. When there is more than one column of text and when these columns are divided by pictures then the reader may lose the direction you want him or her to follow.

FOUR ARTICLES
SEPARATED FROM
EACH OTHER
EACH WITH A CLEAR
READING DIRECTION
BECAUSE OF THICK
RULED LINES

Lines

Lines can be thick or thin, smooth or rough. These differences are easy to achieve and contribute to both clarity and expressiveness.

In the three examples below, the information is separated by lines. This helps clarity. At the same time, the difference between the thickness of the lines contributes to variety and richness of effect.

Note: Thick and thin lines are easy to do on the chalkboard. Just use the side of the chalk for the thick lines! For worksheets have two thicknesses of pen.

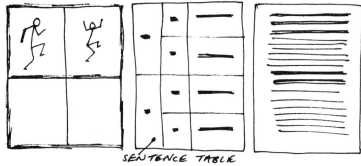

SENTENCE TABLE

THE DIFFERENCE IN LINE THICKNESS HELPS US TO DIFFERENTIATE THE VARIOUS COMPONENTS AND LOOKS NICE

Big and small

Big pictures can be set against a series of small ones. Big titles combined with fine lettering all make for richness of contrast.

Colour

It is tempting to make full use of all the coloured felt tip pens which are available. But it is a little like a teacher trying to win friends by smiling all the time! Students will give little value to the smile after about two minutes if it is unconnected with a communicative reason for smiling.

Colour certainly has an expressive role but how this is achieved can only be judged by the teacher and students. There are two identifiable reasons for using colour for clarity:

Descriptive use of colour

Colour can help us to recognise something. Colour would help us to recognise the difference between an orange, a tomato and a potato.

Diagrammatic use of colour

Colour can be used to draw attention to certain parts of a picture, diagram or text. Perhaps a small present is important in a picture showing several people. If the people are drawn in black and the present is in colour it will attract attention even though it is small.

Tone

Tone is the degree of darkness of a colour. The use of tone can help clarity, recognition and expressiveness.

Clarity

Tonal differences can make shapes easily discernible, for example, the children stand out clearly in the illustration below because of the different tone of the background.
Tone over an area of text helps us to see it as a unity in its own right.

Recognition

Tone may help us to recognise an object. For example, the dark tone of a British policeman's uniform is very characteristic. The tone of cars is not so characteristic because it can vary so much.

Expression

The tone of a design or picture, like music, may be controlled by the amount and relationship of contrasting or harmonising tones. Sharp contrasts will tend to attract attention and be dramatic. Softer tones will offer harmony and gentleness.

Lettering

The teacher can produce a written text by writing, by typing or by using a stencil. Most teachers do not have access to more sophisticated equipment. Here are a few tips arranged according to the basic needs: clarity, recognition and expression.

Clarity

Ability to see what is written depends on the viewer's eyesight, on the size of the letters, on the degree of contrast with the background, on the distance of the viewer and on the illumination.

It is always best to try out any text at the distance you intend using it. However 3 cm is usually a reasonable guide for distances of 10 m.

For projection, many people believe that it is better to have white lettering against a dark background. Computer manufacturers now believe that black lettering on a white screen is the most satisfactory.

Recognition

Recognition of the letters by the form of them depends on familiarity with them. The nearer they are to a familiar form the more readily they will be recognised. An individual handwriting style may present problems. It is better to go for a writing style which is rather like printing.

Expression

Teachers cannot be expected to develop the skills necessary to produce special letters for a variety of expressive purposes. However, in the examples below a few tips for acquiring basic skills will be mentioned.

Tips on writing

The two major contributors to readability are the clarity of the individual letter forms and the distinctive shape of groups of letters in words. Capitals do not give a distinctive shape to a word.

Compare **SHAPE** and shape

Handwriting
For handwriting, a semi-printed form of letter is probably the clearest.

It is recommended that
handwriting be based on
a semi-printed formation
of letters.

A list of tips
Keep your lettering on a horizontal line (usually rubbed out afterwards).
Keep your letters open and clear.
Keep your letters fairly close together.
Keep the upper and lower strokes fairly short.
Keep about two letter's body height between the lines.
Keep the left-hand edge vertical.
Use a lot of ruled lines going right across the grid in order to convey firmness and organisation.

Special titles
It is helpful if you can do a few special types of lettering for titles, particularly for wall displays. The main thing is not to try to do neat and disciplined looking letters.
Fancy styles are easy to do, fast, characterful, eye catching and hide incompetence!

Double pen lettering

Fasten two pens or pencils together. Always hold them at one consistent angle.

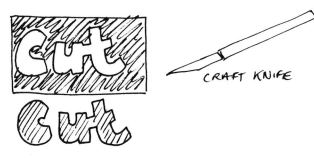

Cutout lettering

A surprisingly successful although slightly more time-consuming technique for displays is to cut out letters with a craft knife from coloured papers. The letters are then stuck down. These letters should be no more than sketched out. Their patently varying character, but with sharp sides and angles, is the secret of their attractiveness and apparent professionalism.

CRAFT KNIFE

Drawing

Tracing

Method 1

If the paper you want to use is thin, then you may be able to see the image to be copied through it. If you can't, then place both the paper with the image on it and the paper to be traced on against the window, preferably with strong sunlight behind. This is the fastest way of tracing.

Alternatively, if you are working at night, put a table lamp on the floor and rest the picture and the paper on a sheet of glass placed above the lamp.

Method 2

Use tracing paper. Trace the picture. Scribble with a soft pencil on the back of the tracing paper. Put the tracing paper down on the area to receive the tracing and draw on top of the tracing.

Enlarging

Method 1
Divide the picture to be copied into squares. Divide the paper you are going to transfer it to into squares. Copy from one square on the picture to a similarly positioned square on the new paper. If the squares on the new paper are twice as big as those on the picture, then the enlargement will be twice as big. The same technique can be used to copy or to reduce a picture. This technique was used by Renaissance painters!

Method 2
Enlarge the picture by epidiascope, or other projector, throwing the image onto the paper you want to use for the copy.

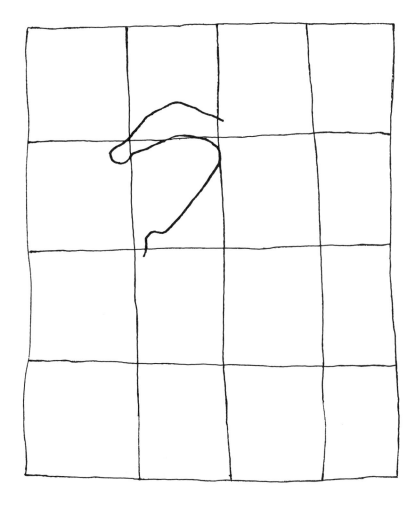

Drawing stickpeople

Which line is longer, a or b?

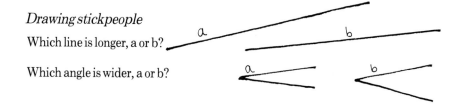

Which angle is wider, a or b?

If you said (a) in both cases you have the necessary talent to draw!
Drawing things so that people can recognise them is basically a matter of
proportions and being able to judge comparative lengths and angles.

Here are the proportions of the basic stickperson.

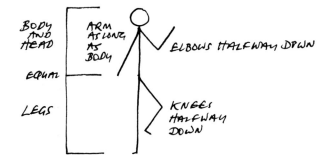

For the sake of speed and the minimising of distracting elements the
stickperson need have no further features, for example, hands, shoulders,
hips, neck. Occasionally it is useful to show the hands.

Here are some badly drawn stickpeople.

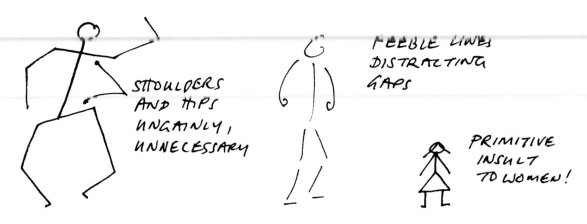

The walking and running stickperson
It is just a matter of getting the angles right.

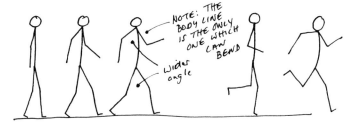

Very slow walking is shown by drawing the arms and legs very near to the vertical. Faster movement is shown by opening the arms and legs out.

Some teachers do not realise that their knees always bend forwards the way they are going and that their elbows point more or less backwards.

Does your stickperson fall over?

The centre of gravity of the body, roughly the abdomen, should be over the supporting point or between the supporting points. Two of the people in the drawing above will fall over. Put in their missing legs to save them!

Noses
Noses are useful because they show which way a stickperson is looking and this might be important if you want to show more than merely an action.

Hands

Usually it is a waste of time to draw the hands. Draw them when you want some special action.

Stickmen, stickwomen and stickchildren

You can show stickwomen easily if you accept the convention of a skirt and long hair. Stickchildren are, obviously, smaller. However, the head is also bigger in proportion. A few characters can be shown.

Copy some of the stickpeople you have seen so far in this book. Practise doing some others.

Boxpeople

There is usually not enough time to draw more than a few lines on the chalkboard. However, you may want to draw 'proper' people on workcards, flashcards, wallpictures or when making figures to use with your magnetboard or flannelboard. These solid figures add interest, give character and increase clarity when seen over a long distance.

And they are no more difficult to draw than stickpeople. If a very simple principle is followed without change nobody need fail!

1 Draw a box for the body, thin if seen from the side and broader if seen from the front.
2 Draw the head.

3 Draw four stick limbs exactly as you would for a stickperson.
4 When step 3 is satisfactory, draw the inside of the legs and arms copying the outside lines more or less exactly.
5 Draw circles for the hands and triangles for the feet.

Because this is a very powerful way of drawing you may be tempted to put in all sorts of bends and flicks to represent clothes and muscles. Any attempt to show more naturalism will expose your limited ability to draw. Nobody is going to say that the triangle is a poor drawing of a foot. So it really is best to stick to the classical boxperson!

Symbols

Symbols can be very useful if they are understood and most of those illustrated here are now internationally known.

Faces

Any bumpy circle will do for a face. (When you want to create special characters you can draw a special shape for the face.) The eyes and nose don't contribute to the expression so put them in first. It is true that large eyes look softer and less aggressive than small eyes.

It is the eyebrows and the mouth which make the expression. Basically, surprise is when the eyebrows are raised. Concentrated thinking is when they are nearer together and nearer to the eyes.

How to turn someone's head
Heads can be turned very easily. Draw the nose in well over to one side. Put the eyes well across as well. The ear is important if you want to turn someone's head; move it across as well.

How to look younger!
Here is the secret. If you want to look younger you must move your features further down your face and make them smaller! In the heads below the overall shape is the same. Note how the nose becomes less pronounced.

Characters

If you can draw a 'normal' face then all you have to do to create a character is to draw a face which is in some way not 'normal'. You can lengthen or shorten the nose. You can place the nose much higher than usual. Or you might like to begin with a different shape to the head, perhaps very square at the bottom and pointed at the top. Whatever you do, you must commit yourself. No half measures!

Animals and objects

Which of these shapes is a London taxi and which is a sports car?

If you are familiar with London taxis you will have said that the first drawing is the taxi and the second the sports car. Every object, however complex its appearance, can be seen as a basic rectangle. The proportions of the rectangle are the essence of its special shape.

Which shape is the horse and which is the cow?

Once you have decided on the object's basic shape you can add those features which will help to make it recognisable. Sometimes you will want to change the outlines away from a rectangle. However, for reasons of speed do this as little as possible. Also try not to be too realistic because then your inexperience in drawing will be revealed.

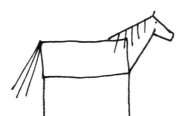

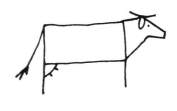

Drawing scenes

When people say they cannot draw they usually mean two things:
1 they cannot draw people naturalistically with all the folds of clothes and the muscles, etc.   2 They cannot draw buildings, cars, etc. in perspective.

In the earlier sections you have seen how to deal with the first self-doubt. The second self-doubt? Don't try to draw perspective! The sort of perspective most people try to draw was only invented in about 1450 in Italy. Many wonderful paintings were done without this Renaissance perspective before 1450 and in other cultures. All you need to do is to flatten everything. Don't show lines disappearing into the distance.
Here is an example for you to copy.

Collage

A rewarding way of making pictures is by collage. Pictures can be drawn or collected by students and combined with writing to make an attractive display.

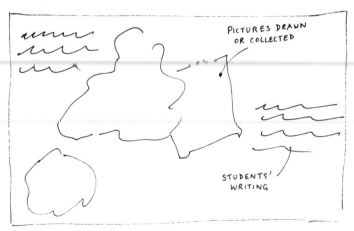

Cutting, sticking and protecting

Cutting

Scissors are useful, of course. However a craft knife is a wonderful help for teachers who want to make their own visual materials.

When cutting out it is advisable to put a piece of thin card under the magazine page.

If you want to cut card with your craft knife do not try to do it at one go. Cut with light strokes again and again.

Metal rulers are useful if you want to cut along a straight line.

Sticking

Paste is cheap. The paper will wrinkle unless you let it expand first. When it has expanded then put it down. As it dries it shrinks and most of the wrinkles should disappear.

Petroleum-based adhesives do not make the paper wrinkle.

Some teachers staple pictures to the backing card.

Protecting

The ideal is to use clear, self-adhesive plastic. It is wonderful if you can tame it! But it seems to have a wilful life of its own. It reaches up and sticks to the wrong part of your workcard, to your sleeve, to the table and worse, to itself. Two ways of dealing with this living creature:
Either
Lay down the plastic sticky side up and drop the workcard on to it. This is all right for small things.
Or
Lay down the workcard image side up. Fold the plastic round like a magazine. Lower the middle onto the middle of the image. Put a ruler through on the inside and slowly press the work out to the outside. Leave enough border to tuck around the back.

The alternative is to tape a clear plastic sheet around the back of the visual or to keep it in a clear plastic envelope.

Displaying

Paste onto hardboard or cardboard and hang up.

Pin or staple to softboard.

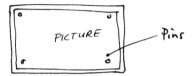

Double sided adhesive tape.

Magnets onto steel strip.

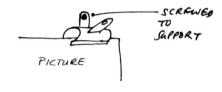

Magnet strip on reverse of picture.

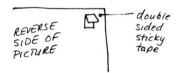

Bulldog clip screwed into support.

Klemboys glued to wall.

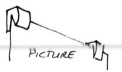

Blu-Tack by Bostik

Wire or string stretched between screws. Bulldog clips for holding the paper.

Further reading

Books about the making and use of visuals

BOWEN, B 1982 *Look Here! Visual Aids in Language Teaching* Macmillan
BYRNE, D 1980 *Using the Magnetboard* Heinemann Educational
HILL, D A 1990 *Visual Impact* Longman
HOLDEN, S (ed) 1973 *Visual Aids for Classroom Interaction* Modern English Publications/Macmillan
JONES, J R H 1982 *Using the Overhead Projector* Heinemann Educational
McALPIN, J 1980 *The Magazine Picture Library* Heinemann Educational
MUGGLESTONE. P 1981 *Planning and Using the Blackboard* Heinemann Educational
SHAW, P and de VET, T 1980 *Using Blackboard Drawing* Heinemann Educational
WRIGHT, A 1984 *1000 Pictures for Teachers to Copy* Collins
WRIGHT, A 1989 *Pictures for Language Learning* Cambridge University Press

Publications making use of visuals which teachers can adapt

BYRNE, D 1986 *Teaching Oral English* (new edition) Longman
BYRNE, D and HALL, D 1976 *Wall Pictures for Language Practice* Longman
HADFIELD, J 1984 *Elementary Communication Games* Nelson
HEATON, J B 1966 *Composition Through Pictures* Longman
KERR, J Y K 1979 *Picture Cue Cards for Oral Language Practice* Nelson
MALEY, A, DUFF, A and GRELLET, F 1980 *The Mind's Eye* Cambridge University Press
MORGAN, J and RINVOLUCRI, M 1983 *Once Upon a Time* Cambridge University Press
SCOTT, W 1980 *Are You Listening?* Oxford University Press
WRIGHT, A 1986 *How to Enjoy Paintings* Cambridge University Press